Parties for Home and School—A Piece of Cake

by
Sandra Lamb
and
Dena Bellows

illustrated by Kathryn Hyndman

Cover by Kathryn Hyndman

Copyright © Good Apple, Inc., 1985

ISBN No. 0-86653-328-1

Printing No. 9876543

GOOD APPLE, INC.
BOX 299
CARTHAGE, IL 62321-0299

Preface

The highlights of a child's school year revolve around celebrations, from Christmas to birthdays and all occasions in between. As adults, many of our fondest memories are festive gatherings with our classmates. An October treat of ice-cream jack-o'-lanterns or valentine fun with Pin the Heart on Raggedy Ann make the magic of childhood memories.

Fast-paced lifestyles and teaching schedules hardly permit time to create the celebrations which are so meaningful to our children. We have collected party ideas that will appeal to teachers and parents of this generation. Our collection ranges from the simple to the more detailed, offering ideas for everyone. You'll find suggestions for party planning from invitations to decorations, the menus and games. As a guide for those wanting a complete party format, we've created a section describing parties based on special themes, perhaps to conclude a unit of study on that topic.

We are indebted to all those teachers and parents who have contributed their ideas. Without their help this book could not have been written. Our experience with our own children's parties has reinforced the need for a party planning manual which will work in the classroom as well as the home. With a few simple guidelines, celebrations can be fun for you and your students.

Introduction

Our book is intended as a guide for you, but most importantly the party is for the child. Design your party with your child's enjoyment in mind; look at a party from your child's point of view, not your own. In other words, don't bring your finest crystal to a preschool party!

No matter how much time, energy and money is invested in your celebration, if it is not carefully planned, the best intentions can result in an unsuccessful party. Try to develop a party plan so that the activities flow smoothly from one event to the next. Keep in mind that a party designed around a theme will be easier to organize and stage. Chances are it will long be remembered.

The book is divided into four general sections. The first part provides guidelines for successful hassle-free party planning. The major focus is specific aspects of party giving, including ideas for invitations, decorations, games and menus. A chapter outlining birthday celebrations from beginning to end follows. This will guarantee smooth sailing from the time invitations go out to the final cleanup. The concluding section presents a potpourri of unique ideas for holiday parties and occasions throughout the year.

The ages we give throughout the book are based on our own experience with our children and suggestions from friends and teachers. Our ideas are meant only as a general guide. Remain flexible and use your imagination to adapt them to your particular party needs and classroom setting.

Our choice to use she to refer to the student was completely unbiased. We drew straws one night and the girls came up victorious.

When specific materials are needed for a project, we have refrained from endorsing brand name products. Craft stores, art supply houses and hardware stores are your best sources for finding supplies you might need. Mail order catalogues frequently offer many unique and hard-to-find items.

As you turn pages we hope you will be caught up in a party spirit and become a child at heart, sharing in the excitement of special celebrations. We hope to decrease your frustration and increase the fun of party giving, providing a loving way to say to your students, ''It's a special day.''

Party Planning

Party Fundamentals

There's nothing like experience. Whether you're a novice or an accomplished party-giver, we all welcome helpful advice. We've gathered some hints to make your occasion hassle-free.

* Let the child help in the planning and encourage her to act as hostess.
* Control the size of the party to avoid chaos—the younger the child, the fewer the guests.
* Extra supervision comes in handy. Parents, baby-sitters, older siblings, relatives are great.
* By the age of four, the party seems to flow more smoothly if every parent does not attend. This helps to make the party child the **only** center of attention.
* Set a reasonable time limit. Except for the very young, two to two and one-half hours is average.
* An outside party is easier on all.
* Don't forget your camera; check flash and purchase extra film.
* Colorful name tags serve as ice-breakers if there are unfamiliar faces.

Children are also aids to supervisors who might not know the whole group.
* To eliminate post party blues, invite one special friend to stay all day.
* Favorite baby-sitters may enjoy being included in the festivities.
* Keep in mind the progression of party events. You should schedule adequate time for eating, playing, and opening gifts. We prefer to open presents early in the party after everyone has arrived. If you decide to wait until later, don't forget kids get tired and people may have to leave early.
* While thank-you notes are a nice gesture, a verbal thanks is adequate for birthday presents. Gifts received through the mail, however, should be acknowledged in writing.

Guidelines for Different Age Groups

For the Youngest: Lots of helping hands should be at the gathering. Don't forget they like to eat, too! This momentous birthday occasion serves as an excuse for a party of relatives and close friends.

Sparkler: Children of this age can be upset by too many unfamiliar faces.

Three or four guests is ideal. Limit the party to one and a half or two hours. They are too young for games, but keep plenty of toys close at hand. Listening to records can be a hit. Children this age tend to play separately. Each child should bring a parent.

Sparkler: To keep things at a child's level, use an old door or a large piece of plywood with a support to each corner. The best height is one and a half feet. No falling off chairs to worry about, but beware of tots crawling up on this novel table!

Preschool: We suggest five guests. The thrill of the occasion is usually enough; however, some simple planned activities can be enjoyed by this group. Coloring, blowing bubbles, playing with clay or blocks, Follow the Leader, simple tossing games, listening to stories or records are some favorites. This age group is interested in shapes and colors. Stimulate this curiosity with a simple game of skill or elementary craft project. Finding like shapes from construction cutouts or creating a masterpiece from a rainbow of colors captivates their attention.

Primary Grades: We recommend four to eight guests. At this age they are ready for supervised games. Keep game instructions to a minimum. If possible, burn off all their excess energy with outdoor games. Some popular games for this group are: Simon Says, Red Light, Follow the Leader, Mother May I, Drop the Handkerchief, Red Rover, Tag, Three-Legged Race, Musical Chairs, Hunts.

Sparkler: To make an event out of the ordinary, create a candlelight lunch or dinner. It's amazing how a little atmosphere makes the food disappear! Everyone loves a fancy fare.

Preventing Accidents

While accidents rarely occur, here are some hazards to beware of.

Balloons: Never allow children to bite them. Balloons can pop, lodge in the throat and even cause suffocation.

Candles: An obvious hazard, but be especially careful of girls with long hair.

Treats on Sticks: Running with lollipops, Popsicles, candy apples, etc., can be very dangerous.

Sparkler: A first-aid kit should be close at hand for emergencies.

Hiring an Entertainer

Hiring a clown, magician or puppeteer is a special treat for all. In order to get the best for your money, keep in mind the following points:

To locate an entertainer, word of mouth is best; otherwise, consult Yellow Pages.

Quality performers are not cheap, but their professionalism guarantees success.

Get as many names as possible and interview each one over the phone.

Listen for signs of confidence, poise, experience and concern.

State ages and sex of the audience.

Responsibilities of the parents include ensuring that the group is punctual, allowing entertainer privacy to set up, providing refreshments and favors, and scheduling time for opening the presents.

Courtesy to the entertainer involves providing suitable place for the show, helping quiet unruly kids, and paying in cash if possible.

INVITATIONS

Remembering the Basics

First impressions do count. Help promote your party with a sensational invitation. However you choose to launch your party, you will need to include the following basic information:

The Occasion
Child's Name
Place
Date
Time (be sure to include an ending time)
R.S.V.P. (by a certain date)
Telephone Number

If mailing the invitations, be sure to do so at least ten to fourteen days before the party. Keep in mind postal restrictions on size and shape of your mailer.

Include on the invitation any special clothing needs, such as bathing suits or costumes. Be sure to mention if the child needs to bring any equipment for the party activities, for example, a doll for a fashion show or a tricycle for a parade. Indicate whether you plan to serve a meal. If parents are to be included at the party, state this on the invitation. This is especially important with the younger set.

Sparkler: Don't pass invites out at school unless you're inviting the whole class. Children get hurt easily and there's no need to make it tough on a sensitive child if she is not to be included.

Clever Ideas for All Occasions

Stationery stores offer a wide selection of attractive invitations which suit many party themes. To personalize your party you may prefer to create your own invitations. Adding original poetry and artwork is especially effective. Even if you are not an artist, clever designs can be achieved by tracing stencils, cookie cutters, or puzzle shapes. We've included a number of unique ideas for homemade invitations.

Original poetry gives a flair to an invitation for any occasion. One birthday idea is to write a poem with party specifics on a number cut out of the child's age. Decorate with stars, glitter, stickers, etc. For other occasions during the year use shapes reminiscent of the holiday. For seasonal parties use: leaf for fall, snowflake for winter, flower for spring, sun for summer.

Numeral Invitation with Poem

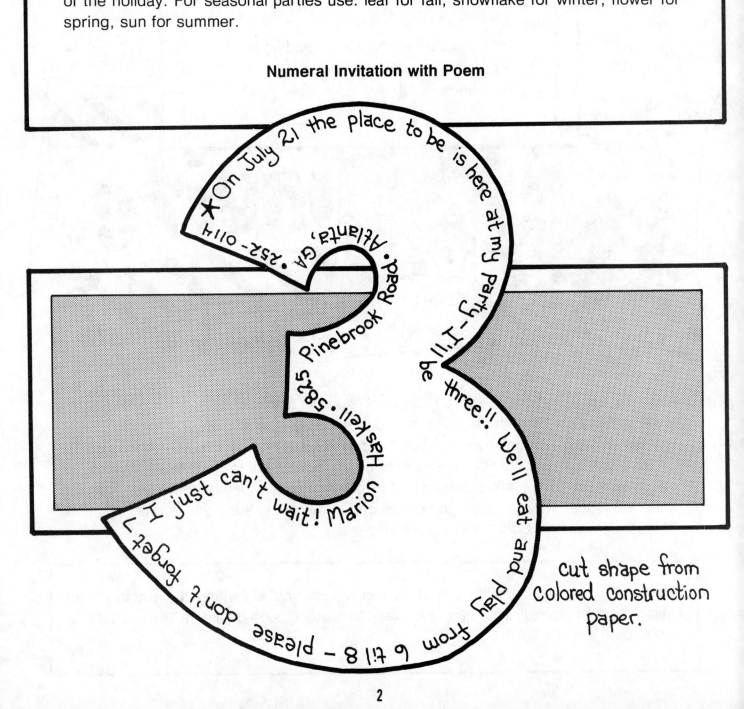

On July 21 the place to be is here at my party - I'll be three!! We'll eat and play from 6 til 8 - please don't forget - I just can't wait! Marion Haskell · 5825 Pinebrook Road · Atlanta, GA · 252-0114

cut shape from colored construction paper.

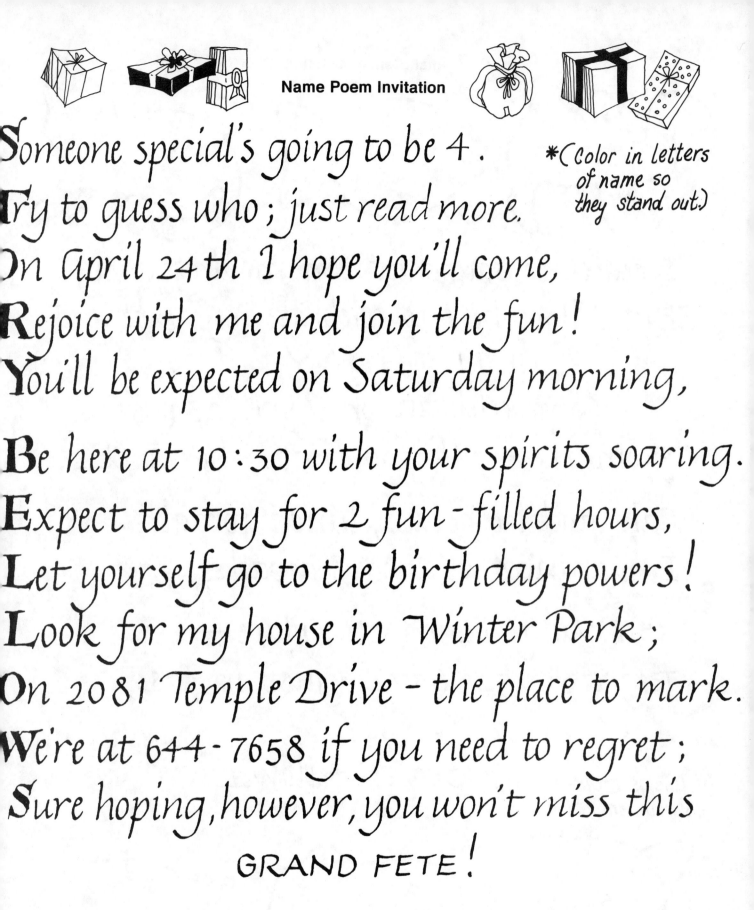

Name Poem Invitation

(Color in letters of name so they stand out.)

Someone special's going to be 4.

Try to guess who; just read more.

On April 24th I hope you'll come,

Rejoice with me and join the fun!

You'll be expected on Saturday morning,

Be here at 10:30 with your spirits soaring.

Expect to stay for 2 fun-filled hours,

Let yourself go to the birthday powers!

Look for my house in Winter Park;

On 2081 Temple Drive - the place to mark.

We're at 644-7658 if you need to regret;

Sure hoping, however, you won't miss this

GRAND FETE!

Your poetry can be attractively written and inexpensively reproduced with a copy machine. Enhance the invitations with glitter, confetti or stickers. Brighten them up with colored markers or pencils. Each student might compose a poem with her own name.

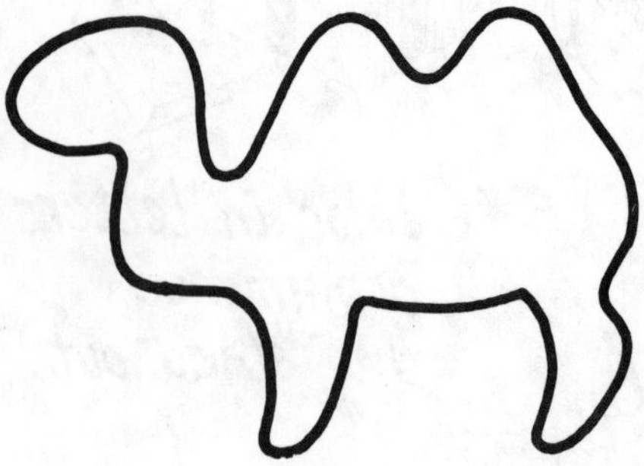

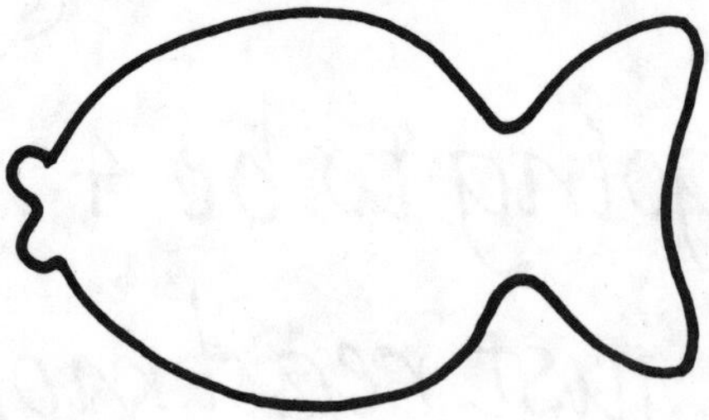

I regret to say that I'm moving away,
But I'll be here to celebrate my sixth
BIRTHDAY !
Come celebrate on April 23 rd;
From 11:30 till 1:00, that's the word.

Cake and ice cream, lunch for all;
I guarantee we'll have a ball.

560 Valley Lane's the place.
Regrets: 252-8572 (just in case).

✳ Story Bellows ✳

*(Use stencils-
Color in animal
      shapes.)

Clever invitations can evolve from imaginative use of common items. Office supply stores are a great place to find interesting forms to send as invitations.

T-shirts (print invitation on front with permanent fabric markers)

Paper Airplanes

Origami Figures

3 x 5 Baggage Tags (Moving Away Party)

Maps (Treasure Hunts, International Party, Moving Away Party)

Airline Tickets (Moving Away Party, International Party)

Report Cards (End of School Party, Graduation Party)

Postcards (They're quick, economical and attention getting. Decorate with colorful markers, decals or crayons.)

Balloons (Blow up and write invitations on them with permanent marker. Let ink dry, deflate balloons and mail in envelopes. Or insert paper invitation inside the balloon and mail. You might even consider delivering the balloons inflated for added drama.)

Jigsaw Puzzle (Make you own jigsaw puzzle from cardboard to which you've glued construction paper. Write party information on the paper; then cut into puzzle pieces. Slip into envelope and mail.)

Brown Lunch Bag (Write party details on one side, fold into thirds and tape closed with colorful sticker. Address the front. These are great for any type of hunt: Easter egg, scavenger, peanut, etc. Invitation doubles as a bag for collecting items.)

Cupcake (Print party information on 3 x 5 cards. Stick corner of card in top of frosted cupcake. Great idea, but does require hand delivery.)

Instead of envelopes consider the following for mailing your invitations:

Diploma Tubes

Toilet Paper Tubes

Paper Towel Tubes

Be sure to tape ends of any mailer to prevent losing invitations.

A Word About R.S.V.P.'s

Children love to receive personal mail, so why not provide R.S.V.P. materials in the invitations to be returned directly to the party child. They should be stamped and self-addressed.

One of our favorites is to include construction cutouts. You will need two shapes for each guest. Place the name of the guest on the front of both shapes; write "Yes" on the back of one and "No" on the back of the second. Responses should be different colors. Guest returns the appropriate reply.

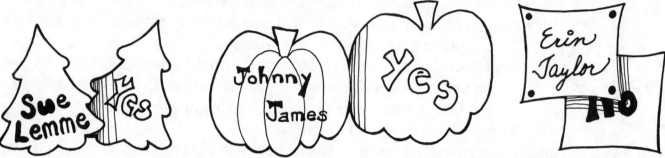

For birthday parties use a shape suggestive of your party theme, such as an animal shape for a circus party. Shapes for other parties are tree or Santa face for Christmas, pumpkin for Halloween or heart for Valentine's Day. You can always use simple circles or squares for your cutout.

An enclosed postcard with "yes" or "no" check boxes would work as well. This is quicker to make and cheaper to return.

You may want to attach R.S.V.P.'s to a poster board. This lets the child know who can and cannot attend; it also builds excitement for the event.

DECORATIONS

Making It Festive

What's a party without balloons! Let the world know there's a celebration. Float balloons from your mailbox, lamppost, front door, even a tree. Make sure to have plenty indoors. You can order helium balloons from some florist and speciality shops or try renting a helium tank from a welding shop, hospital rental or party supply house to blow up your own. Mylar balloons are the most dramatic and stay up longer.

Sparkler: Party balloons will stick to the ceiling if you rub them first against wool.

Place Cards

While not essential, place cards provide a warm welcome for your guests and eliminate any potential bickering. Some simple ideas are:

* Polaroid Pictures (Take a picture of each guest as she enters. Place the picture at her place.)
* Personalized Favors (mugs, barrettes, boxes, etc.)
* Balloons (Fill with helium and tie with a string to back of each chair. Be sure to write name across each balloon.
  Or stand a long skinny balloon in a paper cup at each child's place. Write her name across it and decorate with a face. You can tape yarn to top for hair.)

* Tiny Baskets (Fill with colorful jellybeans or any holiday candies wrapped in cellophane. Label each with child's name.)
* Shoe Mates (Prior to the party, write children's names on masking tape. Before serving the meal, have each child take off one shoe and tape her name to the bottom. Put a shoe at each party place. The challenge is to locate the correct place setting by matching mates.)

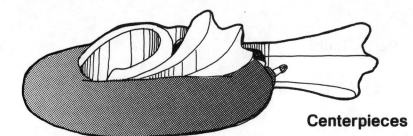

Centerpieces

An unusual centerpiece helps create a spectacular party table. We think these are dynamite.

* Jack Horner Pie: Decorate a box appropriately for your occasion: treasure chest, pumpkin, cake, animal, rocket, truck, etc. Wrap a small gift for each guest and tie a ribbon to it. Place all gifts inside the centerpiece and let ribbon reach to each child's place. When the signal is given, children pull ribbons and unwrap their favors.

* Stuffed Animals or Dolls: They're readily available and look really adorable. Why not let Snoopy hold a helium balloon!

* Goldfish Bowl: Dazzle their eyes with real fish swimming at the center of your table. You can even put goldfish in large brandy snifters.

* Commercial Paper Centerpieces

* Use plain paper cloths on the table. Give each guest 1 or 2 crayons to create a masterpiece while waiting to be served.

* Balloons: A cascade of them hung over the table.

* Any object you have pertaining to the party theme will make a good centerpiece. For a space party use a toy rocket ship; for a swimming party try flippers and goggles; for Halloween use a carved pumpkin containing dry ice.

Don't forget your birthday cake can double as a centerpiece; however, it won't survive until the troops disperse!

Other focal points of your table might include draping your table with different colored crepe paper rather than a cloth, sprinkling confetti along table top, or enthroning the birthday child by decorating her chair with greenery, ribbons, flowers, balloons, etc., and making a special crown or flower corsage.

Party Room

Ideally, decorations should be suited to your party theme. These decorating tips will add spark to any party room.

Homemade Banner: Include names of all guests. Write or paint these colorful greetings on muslin, burlap, canvas, poster board or butcher paper. Use glue and glitter on burlap or felt. Use dowel to secure banner and display in a prominent place.

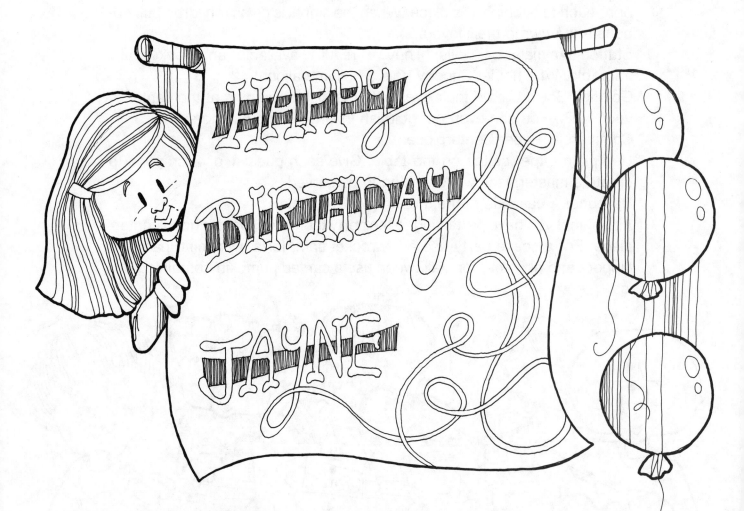

Kites: These colorful sails are very festive when hung from the ceiling and attached to the walls.

Photo Blow-Up: These posters take time to order, and you decide if it's worth the added expense. We'll guarantee gales of laughter if you select a comical pose.

Ceiling Fan: Hang colorful strands of crepe paper from blades of the fan. Use different colors cut to various lengths and turn the fan on low. This calliope of colors intrigues the younger set.

FAVORS AND PRIZES

Avoiding Arguments

Prizes and favors are an integral part of every celebration. To avoid squabbles, review the following pointers:

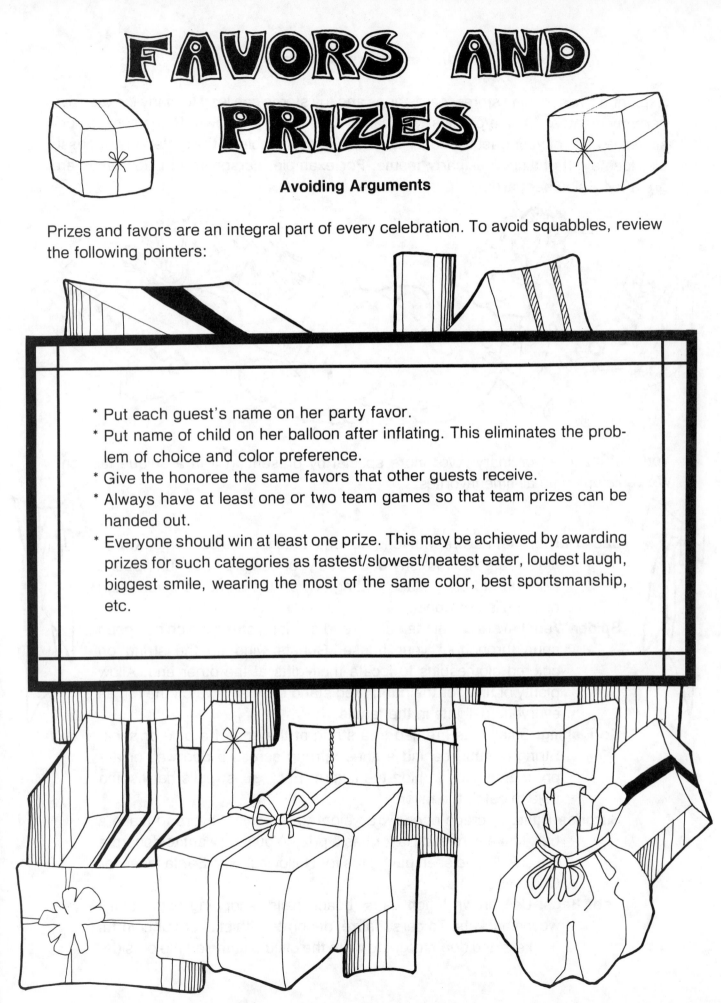

* Put each guest's name on her party favor.
* Put name of child on her balloon after inflating. This eliminates the problem of choice and color preference.
* Give the honoree the same favors that other guests receive.
* Always have at least one or two team games so that team prizes can be handed out.
* Everyone should win at least one prize. This may be achieved by awarding prizes for such categories as fastest/slowest/neatest eater, loudest laugh, biggest smile, wearing the most of the same color, best sportsmanship, etc.

Unique Favors and Prizes

Exploring five and dime stores, card shops and toy stores can lead to many inexpensive party mementoes. If time permits, you can always make your own. Remember to consider the ages of your guests and try to select items suitable to their interests. If possible, locate gifts fitting your party theme. For example, personalized pillowcases are great for a slumber party.

You can make an ordinary favor more special by presenting it in a unique fashion. We've listed some all-time favorites.

Jack Horner Pie: Favors with long ribbons attached are concealed within a decorated box which doubles as your centerpiece. Run ribbons from box to each place setting. When the signal is given each child pulls her ribbon.

Spider Web: Favors are hidden at the end of a long string which has been spun throughout your house. Guests wind up the string on colored clothespins to locate their gifts at the other end. Allow plenty of time for the hunt; then stand back and watch the fun as everyone delights in the tangle.

Go Fishing: Small gifts are tied to a string at the end of a pole or stick. String is hung behind a sheet strung across a doorway or appropriate space to hide the favors. Each guest pulls her fishing pole to catch the favor.

Surprise Balls: In crepe paper wrap eight to ten small favors to make a ball. Make sure each layer has a prize. You may want to decorate the ball. We've seen pumpkins for Halloween and Santa faces for Christmas.

Loot Bags: Use brown lunch bags, beach pails, shopping bags, small woven baskets. To personalize, decorate with stickers or colorful markers and don't forget to write the child's name on the outside.

For some unusual favors consider the following:

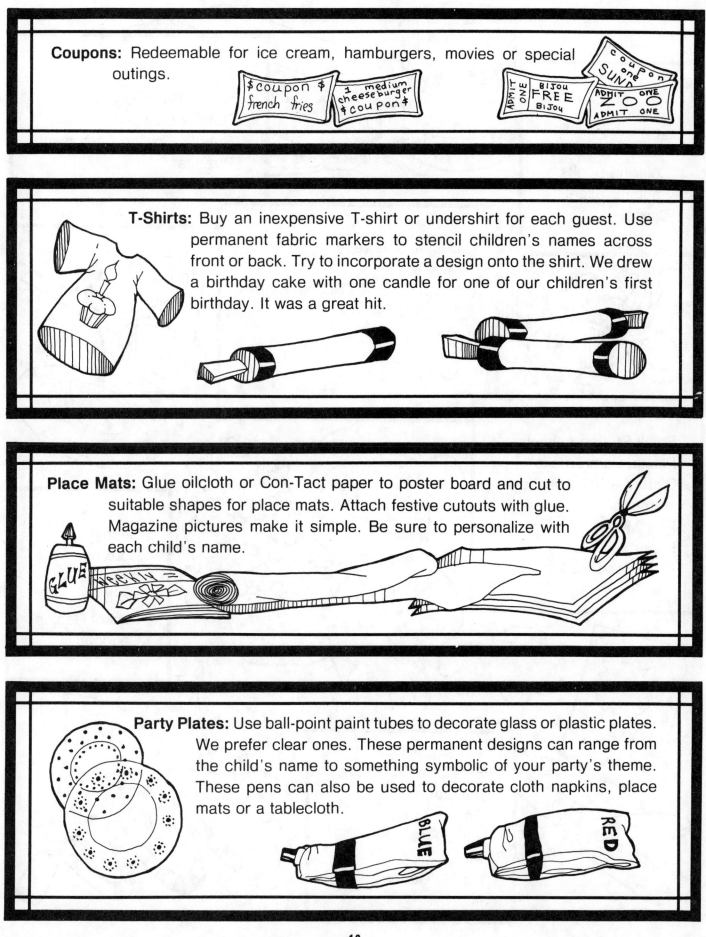

Coupons: Redeemable for ice cream, hamburgers, movies or special outings.

$coupon $
french fries

1 medium
cheeseburger
$coupon$

coupon
one
SUND
ZOO

ADMIT
ONE

BIJOU
FREE
BIJOU

ADMIT ONE

ADMIT ONE

T-Shirts: Buy an inexpensive T-shirt or undershirt for each guest. Use permanent fabric markers to stencil children's names across front or back. Try to incorporate a design onto the shirt. We drew a birthday cake with one candle for one of our children's first birthday. It was a great hit.

Place Mats: Glue oilcloth or Con-Tact paper to poster board and cut to suitable shapes for place mats. Attach festive cutouts with glue. Magazine pictures make it simple. Be sure to personalize with each child's name.

GLUE

Party Plates: Use ball-point paint tubes to decorate glass or plastic plates. We prefer clear ones. These permanent designs can range from the child's name to something symbolic of your party's theme. These pens can also be used to decorate cloth napkins, place mats or a tablecloth.

BLUE

RED

Favorite Favors

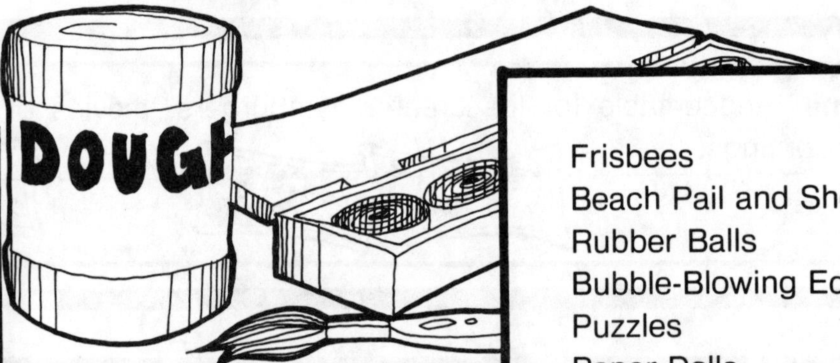

Play-Doh
Crayons/Pencils
Watercolors
Coloring Books
Fancy Erasers
Cards

Frisbees
Beach Pail and Shovel
Rubber Balls
Bubble-Blowing Equipment
Puzzles
Paper Dolls

Costume Jewelry
Makeup
Soap/Shampoo/Bubble Bath
Sunglasses
Sun Visors
Jacks
Marbles

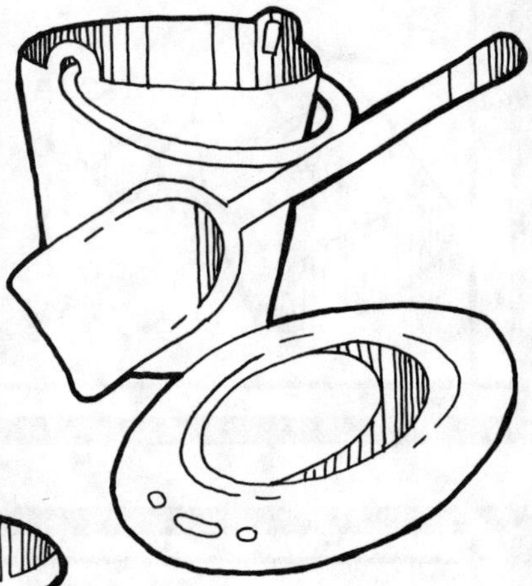

Small Stuffed Animals
Plastic Cars/Trucks
Gliders—Wood or Plastic
Magnets
Play Money
Paperback Books
Plant Seed Packets

Candy
Cookies
Whistles
Horns
Pocket Games
Coupons

Small Plastic Games
Bandanas
Comic Books
Jump Rope
Kite
Cookie Cutter

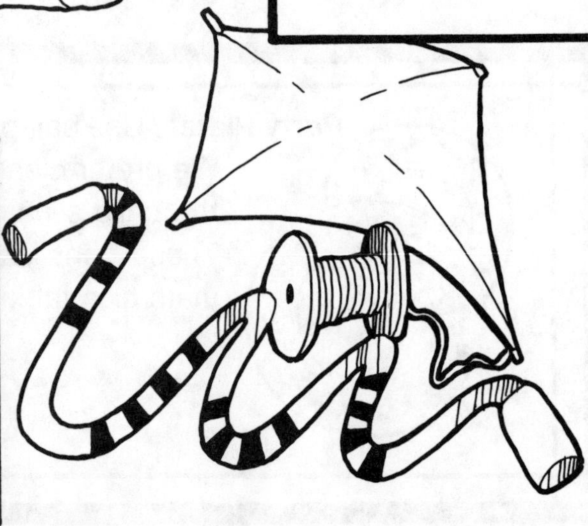

GIFTS

Unique Wrappings

Appearance is important. Why not spruce up your packages with clever wrappings!

Comic Strip Pages
Chinese or Japanese Newspapers
Wallpaper—leftovers, of course!
Sheet Music
Fabric Scraps
Disposable Diapers (for baby gifts)
Road Maps
Original Artwork

Instead of ribbon try:
    Heavy Duty Twines
    Fabric Cut into Strips
    Lace Hem Bindings
    Yarns
    Rickrack

To decorate the tops of packages use:
    Fresh, Pressed or Dried Flowers
    Seashells
    Herb Sprigs
    Feathers
    Small Toy
    Lollipops
    Small Balloons

To conceal large items consider:
    Plastic Garbage Bags
    Paper Tablecloth
    An Old Sheet

For a tiny item such as money or jewelry, we recommend a matchbox covered with wrapping paper.
If boxes are not available, coffee cans, tennis ball cans, any aluminum can with a plastic lid make great containers. Wrap them and top with ribbons.
Egg cartons have great compartments for hiding coins, golf balls, any small items such as matchbox cars, barrettes, jewelry. Cut the carton in half for six items.
Cushion a fragile gift for mailing in plain popped popcorn.

Family Traditions

Birthdays are a perfect time to establish a tradition that will delight your child each year. The added effort will not go unnoticed.

* Give a child a tree, flower or bush: azaleas, bulbs, or flowering trees—a living thing to grow right along with your child.
* The measuring door celebrates another year's growth with a record of your child's height on the door jamb. Label marks with dates. If you move, measure marks, record and transfer to your new home.
* Create a hand wreath. Make a pattern by tracing your child's handprint onto construction paper. Shape into a wreath by gluing or stapling. Take out each year to compare growth. Rather than a new wreath each year, you may choose to build one wreath with each year's handprint added until the wreath is complete.

green
paper

red
paper

green
paper

Trace child's handprint onto red & green construction paper. Glue or staple alternating colors around a circle to form a wreath. Decorate with a festive ribbon.

Hand Wreath

A special candle may be burned only on birthdays for a short time. Make certain it is large enough to last through many celebrations.

Tablecloth: An ambitious soul might want to write with permanent markers or stitch the names of each year's party guests onto a tablecloth. Pull out this piece of history each year on the special day. You may want to trace handprints of guests as well. Incidentally, sheets make great tablecloths.

Birthday Bulletin: On the day a child is born, save a copy of the newspaper. Present it to your child when she is old enough to enjoy it. Why not save each year's birthday news? Don't forget horoscopes.

Birthday Letter: Parents, grandparents or special people may want to compose a letter recording high points of the birthday child's past year. Tuck the letter in along with the gift and when the birthday is over, the letter is kept. These will be cherished in the years to come.

Future Investment: Each year give your child an amount of money corresponding to her age. You might consider opening a birthday account to be added to on each birthday. To add an element of surprise, wrap the money in foil and hide it somewhere in the birthday dinner.

Silver dollars are a special treat to receive from year to year. Hide one or two in a special place each year.

Books and Such: Start a library for your child of distinctive books or records. Personalized bookplates create a nice touch.

Instead of a gift give a special service: plant a garden, cook a special fare, build a project. As an alternative give a special occasion: a weekend trip, tickets to the movies, or dinner out with a friend.

Add to a collection: china, silver, stamps, soldiers, books, coins, etc.

Gifts for Friends

Say it with balloons. You can't miss with these festive bouquets.

* Present a child with a bouquet of helium-filled balloons. This may be rather expensive, but we think it is worth it in the fun it creates for the kids. Make sure there are enough to go around.
* Hide a dollar bill in a balloon. Mail it along with a card and instructions to blow up and pop. Other enclosures might be gum, candy, barrettes, necklaces, or coupons for treats.

18

MENU

While feasting is a traditional part of most parties, the fare does not have to be elaborate. The key to success is to prepare ahead whenever possible: make sandwiches, scoop the ice cream (put in paper cups or on paper plates in freezer), pour drinks, etc. This menu section is intended to give the party host and hostess a few simple hints on easy edibles for the young and some clever presentations for party fares. Detailed menus are included under the thematic party section.

Creative Adaptions for Any Holiday

To make the food at a holiday party more festive, remember these easy tricks:

Sandwiches: Use cookie cutter shapes appropriate to the holiday and decorate accordingly.
> Heart—Valentine's Day
> Star, Bell, Tree, Santa—Christmas
> Rabbit— Easter

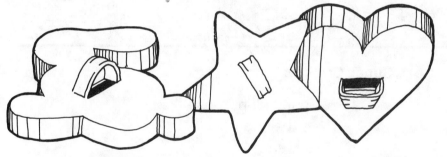

Amazing Ices: Freeze fruits or holiday candies inside ice cubes, then float in the beverages. Heart candies for Valentine's Day, candy corn for Halloween, etc. Make sure you try this ahead of time to be sure the dye in your candy will hold up during freezing. Red candy coloring does not seem to work.

Jell-O Molds: Jell-O can be gelled into individual molds or cut with cookie cutters from a shallow pan once the Jell-O has thoroughly set (use a spatula to remove). Again, use shapes reminiscent of the holiday.

Cookies: Use shapes for holidays or numbers for birthdays to cut popular sugar cookies. Here's a basic recipe and frosting mix.

COOKiES

Sugar Cookies

¾ cup shortening
1 cup sugar
2 eggs
1 tsp. vanilla

2½ cups all-purpose flour
1 tsp. baking powder
½ tsp. salt
frosting

Cream shortening; gradually add sugar, beating until fluffy. Add eggs and vanilla; mix well. Combine dry ingredients; add to creamed mixture, mixing well. Divide dough in half; wrap in waxed paper and chill at least 1 hour. Roll ½ of the dough to ¼'' thickness on a lightly floured surface. Keep remaining dough chilled. Cut dough with a cookie cutter. Place on greased cookie sheets; bake at 350° for 12 minutes or until edges are lightly browned. Cool cookies on a wire rack. Repeat with remaining dough. Frost if desired.

Frosting

6 tbsp. butter or margarine, softened
¼ cup milk
food coloring (optional)

1 (16 oz.) pkg. powdered sugar, sifted
1 tsp. vanilla

Cream butter, gradually add sugar, beating until well-blended. Add milk and vanilla, mixing until smooth. Stir in food coloring, if desired. Frosting for 3 dozen cookies.

The Meal

We've included a general list of all-time favorites, followed by a few unique tempting treats.

Favorites

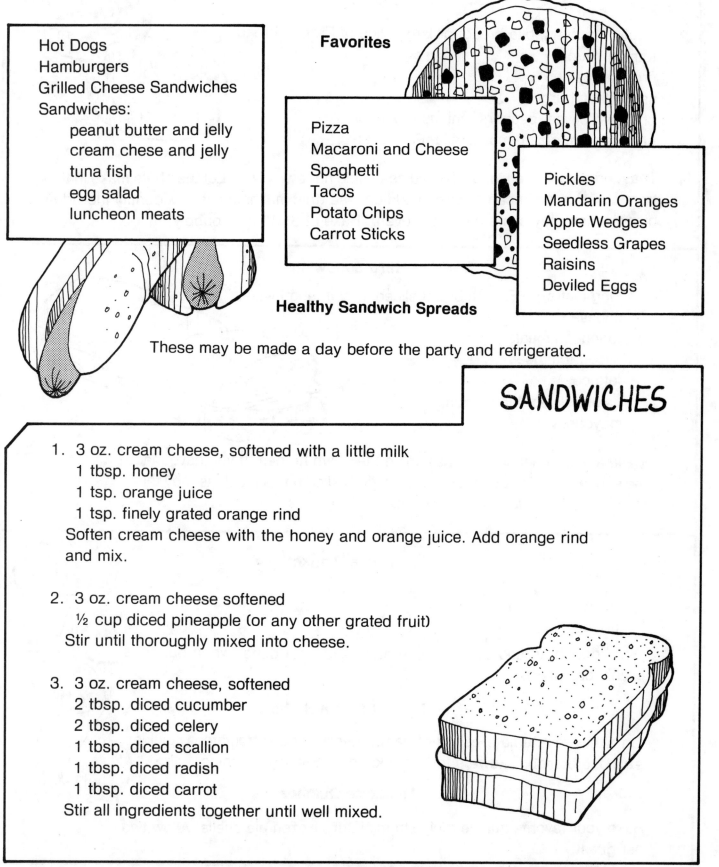

Hot Dogs
Hamburgers
Grilled Cheese Sandwiches
Sandwiches:
  peanut butter and jelly
  cream chese and jelly
  tuna fish
  egg salad
  luncheon meats

Pizza
Macaroni and Cheese
Spaghetti
Tacos
Potato Chips
Carrot Sticks

Pickles
Mandarin Oranges
Apple Wedges
Seedless Grapes
Raisins
Deviled Eggs

Healthy Sandwich Spreads

These may be made a day before the party and refrigerated.

SANDWICHES

1. 3 oz. cream cheese, softened with a little milk
   1 tbsp. honey
   1 tsp. orange juice
   1 tsp. finely grated orange rind
   Soften cream cheese with the honey and orange juice. Add orange rind and mix.

2. 3 oz. cream cheese softened
   ½ cup diced pineapple (or any other grated fruit)
   Stir until thoroughly mixed into cheese.

3. 3 oz. cream cheese, softened
   2 tbsp. diced cucumber
   2 tbsp. diced celery
   1 tbsp. diced scallion
   1 tbsp. diced radish
   1 tbsp. diced carrot
   Stir all ingredients together until well mixed.

Personal Pizzas

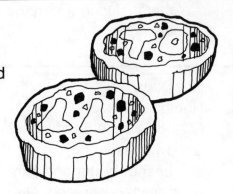

English muffins, pita bread, or large slice of French bread
tomato sauce
oregano/basil
salami/hamburger
chopped olives, peppers, onions (optional)
cheese—American, mozzarella, Parmesan

Toast bread and then let each child assemble her own pizza. Let the chefs make initials from slices of American or mozzarella cheese (this makes it easy to identify individual pizzas when they come out of the oven). Bake at 350° until bubbly.

Hero Sandwich

long loaf(s) of French bread sliced in half lengthwise.
cheese
luncheon meats
sliced tomatoes
lettuce
onion, sliced thin (optional)
mayonnaise

Make ahead or let children assemble their own heroes. If you have made the sandwiches in advance, let the children slice off as much as they think they'll eat. Great for slumber parties.

Pigs in a Blanket

canned roll dough
hot dogs

Wrap dough around the hot dogs and bake until done (when dough is evenly browned).

Picnic Shish Kebobs

On skewers alternate cubes of ham, cheese, cherry tomatoes, pickles, etc. Use bamboo skewers for small kebobs. Serve with chips.

Miniature Quiches

Bake your favorite quiche recipe in miniature frozen pie shells. Allow two per guest.

Create Your Own Sandwich

Provide luncheon meats and fillings for chefs to create their own sandwiches. Let each child use cookie cutters to cut bread and meat; then let the artists in them take over! Put out raisins, lettuce, carrots, pickles, olives, etc., so each chef can create a masterpiece—an animal, person, face, whatever. Let children vote on the funniest, most realistic, etc.

Guess My Shape

For the very young crowd, you might want to cut sandwiches into various shapes—circles, triangles, squares, etc. Give each child two different sandwiches and have the children guess who has a diamond, square, etc.

Bread

Filling in Middle

Bread

Use cookie cutter or make your own pattern for numbers.

Number Sandwiches

Cut sandwiches in the shape of the number corresponding with the child's age. Use creamy fillings such as peanut butter and jelly or cream cheese. These are a great hit.

Perfect Presentations

To present your picnic fare, try one of these novel ideas.

* Paper lunch bags decorated with stickers and child's name.

* Chinese take-out containers decorated with anything reminiscent of the party theme and identified with child's name.

* Plastic beach bucket personalized with child's name and stuffed with luncheon goodies!

BEVERAGES

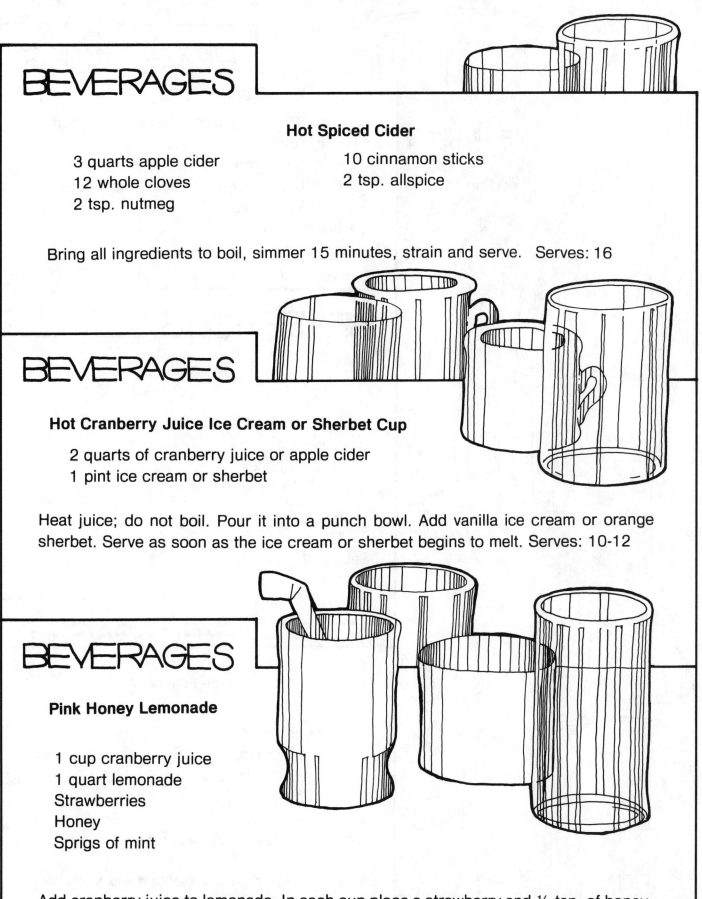

Hot Spiced Cider

3 quarts apple cider
12 whole cloves
2 tsp. nutmeg

10 cinnamon sticks
2 tsp. allspice

Bring all ingredients to boil, simmer 15 minutes, strain and serve.   Serves: 16

BEVERAGES

Hot Cranberry Juice Ice Cream or Sherbet Cup

2 quarts of cranberry juice or apple cider
1 pint ice cream or sherbet

Heat juice; do not boil. Pour it into a punch bowl. Add vanilla ice cream or orange sherbet. Serve as soon as the ice cream or sherbet begins to melt. Serves: 10-12

BEVERAGES

Pink Honey Lemonade

1 cup cranberry juice
1 quart lemonade
Strawberries
Honey
Sprigs of mint

Add cranberry juice to lemonade. In each cup place a strawberry and ¼ tsp. of honey. Do this step before the party begins. Then add juice and decorate with a sprig of mint.

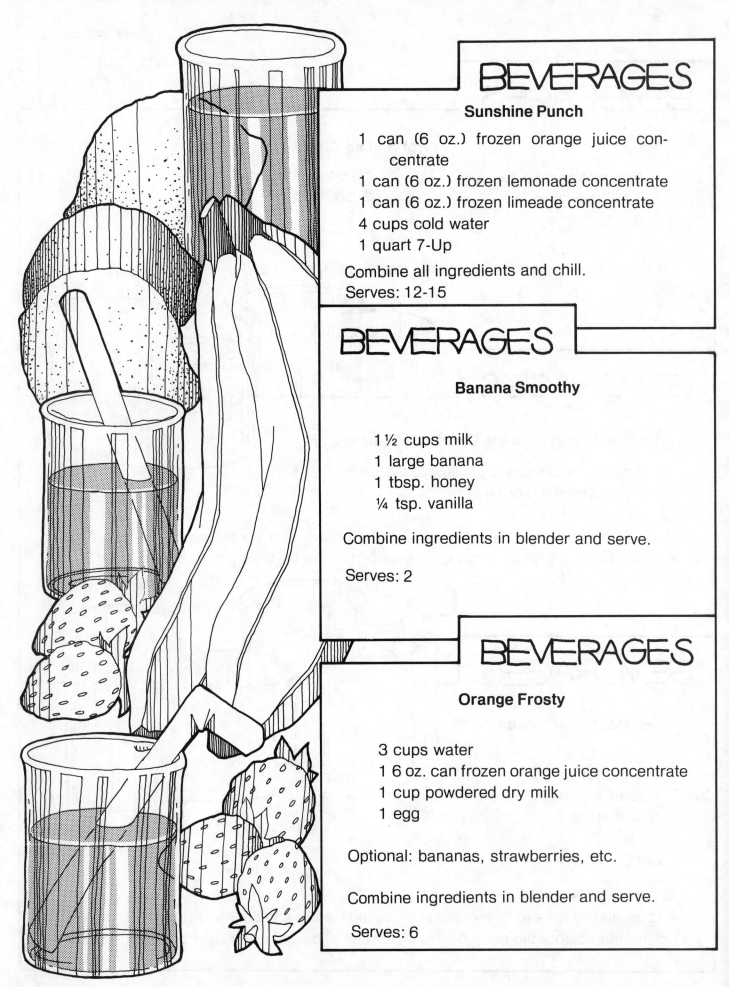

BEVERAGES

Sunshine Punch

1 can (6 oz.) frozen orange juice concentrate
1 can (6 oz.) frozen lemonade concentrate
1 can (6 oz.) frozen limeade concentrate
4 cups cold water
1 quart 7-Up

Combine all ingredients and chill.
Serves: 12-15

BEVERAGES

Banana Smoothy

1 ½ cups milk
1 large banana
1 tbsp. honey
¼ tsp. vanilla

Combine ingredients in blender and serve.

Serves: 2

BEVERAGES

Orange Frosty

3 cups water
1 6 oz. can frozen orange juice concentrate
1 cup powdered dry milk
1 egg

Optional: bananas, strawberries, etc.

Combine ingredients in blender and serve.

Serves: 6

Cakes

A festive cake is the highlight of every party. You don't need to be a professional to create a special cake in your own kitchen. With your favorite recipe or packaged mix and a little imagination, you can achieve terrific results.

Our thematic party section includes many ideas for both ice cream and cakes. These ideas will make any cake spectacular.

Candy stores are the perfect places to find colorful, edible decorations for your cake. Spell out your message in chocolate morsels, miniature marshmallows, red cinnamon candies or M & M's; make outlines with licorice rope; add drama with gumdrops, jellybeans, chocolate kisses, marshmallows, or lollipops. Candies are also great for creating facial features: eyes—chocolate chips, M & M's; ears—chocolate kisses, jellybeans, red cinnamon candies, raisins; nose—gumdrops, marshmallows; mouth—licorice, red cinnamon candies; hair or fur—dyed coconut.

Miniatures are available in great variety. Use them on top of your cake to help carry out the party theme.

Candleholders can be made with Life Savers or miniature marshmallows.

Colored icing creates a lot of excitement. Mix food coloring with any white frosting.

AND OTHER TREATS

Coconut can be dyed any color.

  ½ teaspoon milk or water
  Few drops of food coloring
  1 ⅓ cups flake coconut

Mix milk and food coloring in a bowl. Add coconut and toss with a fork until coconut is evenly tinted.

Frost a design by cutting a stencil from cardboard or use a paper doily. Place stencil on cake and frost. Carefully remove stencil. A cowboy cut-out is great for a Western party. We found a precut stencil set in a gourmet shop. (See Supply List.)

There is no need to purchase expensive cake pans; almost any shape can be cut from either a round or a rectangular pan. Make sure cake is completely cool before cutting and mark the cake with wooden picks before actually cutting. You can use a cutout paper pattern. After cutting, first frost pieces together to hold; then frost all cut edges, leaving tops and uncut edges for last.

Create a cake full of surprises by baking coins wrapped in foil inside.

Kids love candles which extinguish and then relight after blowing out.

We have found long thin candles which look fantastic on a cake and burn for 25 minutes.

For the Very Young

If you want to avoid a "sugar high," make a festive Jell-O mold and add a candle for that special day. You will not be able to get away with it as the children get older!

A "baby cake" or cupcake will keep the very young occupied while you serve the larger cake to older guests.

Instead of the traditional cake, place cupcakes on a tray in the numerical shape of the child's age. Place a candle in each. No waiting for the cake to be cut.

Cupcake Number Shape

Serve on a tray or baking sheet.

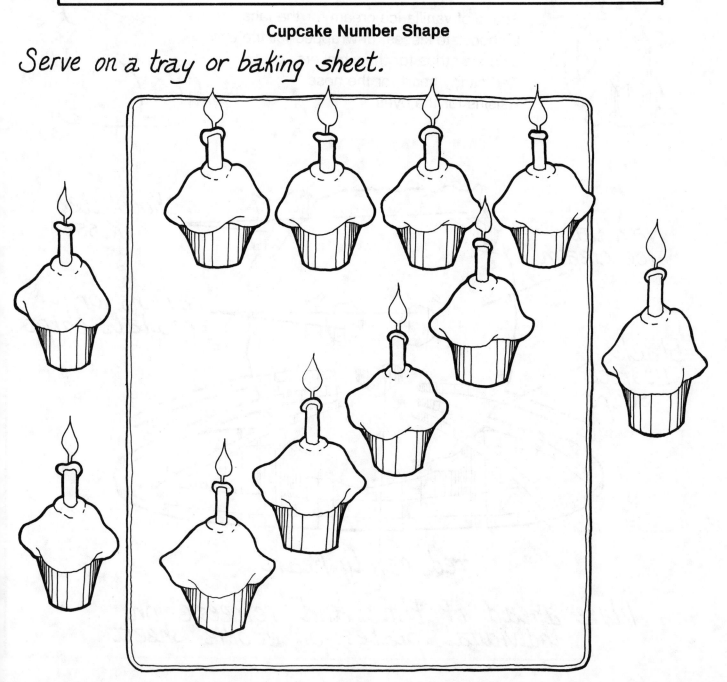

29

Ice Cream

Why not dress up your ice cream for the party? To save time on the party day, scoop ice cream beforehand into balls and refreeze on a cookie sheet. When refreshment time comes, simply remove the scoops from the freezer and place on individual plates.

Sparkler: For children with milk allergies, keep Cool Whip in the freezer. It becomes their own special ice cream.

Ice-Cream Kitten

Scoop of vanilla ice cream for the face
2 chocolate kisses, unwrapped for the ears
Licorice strips for the whiskers
Red candy heart for the nose
Raisins for the eyes

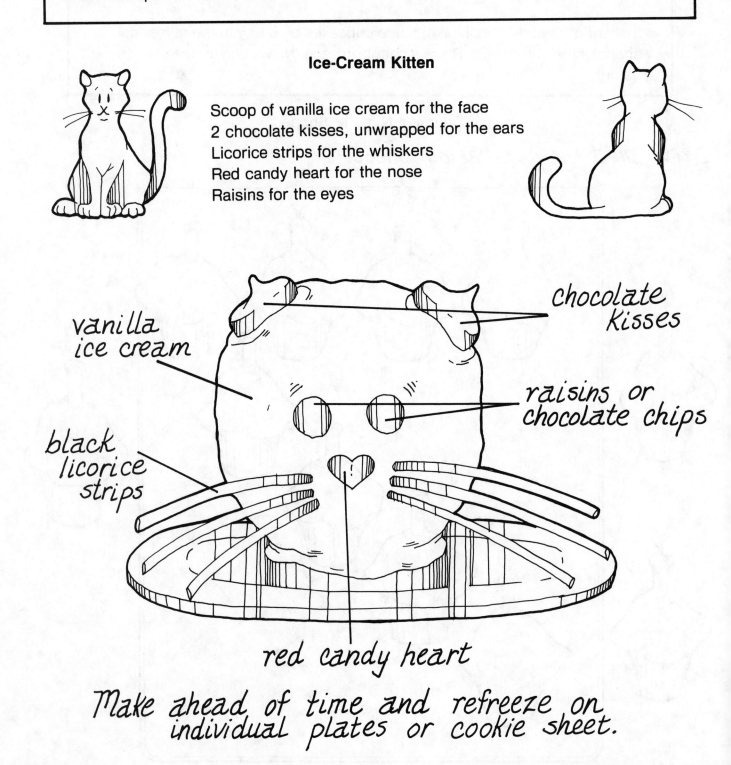

vanilla ice cream

chocolate kisses

black licorice strips

raisins or chocolate chips

red candy heart

Make ahead of time and refreeze on individual plates or cookie sheet.

Snowballs: These are great for a winter party. Roll scoops of ice cream in coconut flakes and refreeze. You might consider using small scoops to form a snowman. Decorate his face with chocolate chips for the eyes, a carrot slice for the nose and red licorice for the mouth.

Green Thumb Ice Cream

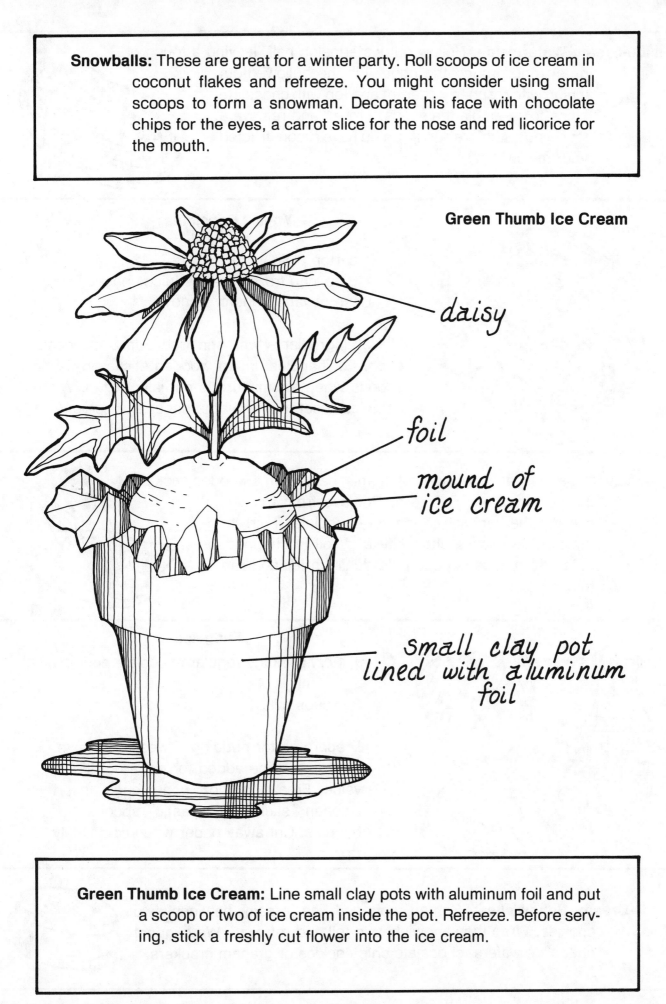

daisy

foil

mound of ice cream

small clay pot lined with aluminum foil

Green Thumb Ice Cream: Line small clay pots with aluminum foil and put a scoop or two of ice cream inside the pot. Refreeze. Before serving, stick a freshly cut flower into the ice cream.

Ice-Cream Watermelon: Hollow out watermelon half, leaving a touch of green rind around the edge. Fill the hollowed-out melon with raspberry sherbet and top with chocolate chips to resemble the seeds. Freeze and remove a few minutes before serving. You have reconstructed your melon.

Yogurt Popsicles

1 carton plain yogurt
1 6 oz. can frozen orange juice concentrate
Dash of vanilla and/or honey

Mix all ingredients well and freeze in 3 oz. paper cups. For handles, insert wooden sticks or plastic spoons when the mixture is partially frozen. When completely set, cut away the paper and serve.

Banana Pops: Peel bananas and cut them in half. Push a wooden stick up the center of each. Freeze. Remove from freezer and dip the bananas in melted chocolate. Twirl to remove the excess chocolate and roll in chopped nuts. Wrap banana pops individually in foil and re-freeze.

Fudgsicles

1 4 oz. package regular chocolate pudding
          mix
3½ cups milk

Prepare as for pudding. Sweeten to taste. An egg may be added for extra nutritional value. Freeze in 3 oz. paper cups. Insert wooden sticks or plastic spoons for handles. Cut away paper when completely frozen.

Ice-Cream Sandwiches: Spread softened ice cream between two cookies. Wrap the sandwiches in foil and refreeze. We suggest chocolate wafers, chocolate chip cookies or graham crackers.

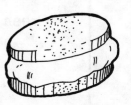

Cone Cupcakes: Prepare cake mix per package instructions. Pour batter into flat bottom ice-cream cones. Place each cone inside the hole of a muffin pan to be sure they do not tip over. Fill up enough so that the batter will rise up out of the cone, about halfway, to resemble an ice-cream cone. Bake at 350° for 20-25 minutes. Cool, frost and place a candle on top.

Number Cookies: Mold cookie dough into number shape corresponding with your child's age. Number cookie cutters are also available. Bake, frost with a tinted sugar frosting, and let the world in on how old the birthday child is.

Name Cookies: Mold cookie dough in letter shapes to spell out children's names. Bake and serve.

Create a Cupcake: Give each child an unfrosted cupcake or two, a small dish of frosting, and a knife (not too sharp). Place various toppings within reach and let the cake decorators go to work. Use colored sugars, jimmies, M & M's, chopped nuts and gumdrops.

GAMES

Miscellaneous Tips

At an early age, children learn that games are the highlight of many party celebrations. Whether your party is indoors or out, we have collected an array of ideas to keep your group busy and happy. Before you plan any games, however, remember a few simple guidelines.

Prizes are a must. They should be wrapped. A quick wrap: place prize in a small paper bag and tie the bag with a bright ribbon. Everyone should win at least one prize. Towards the end of the party, award prizes to those who did not win any games. Make up prize categories: fastest eater, biggest smile, loudest laugh, best sportsmanship, wearing the most of one color, etc.

Try to have at least one or two team games so that team prizes can be handed out.

Suggestions for prize categories for relay games (these are designed so you can have more than one winner):

  Running—runs as fast as a racehorse, deer, jet, race car
  Jumping—jumps as high as the moon, a kangaroo, a super frog
  Catching—catches or throws as well as _____(name a major league baseball player)
  Climbs—climbs like a monkey, spider

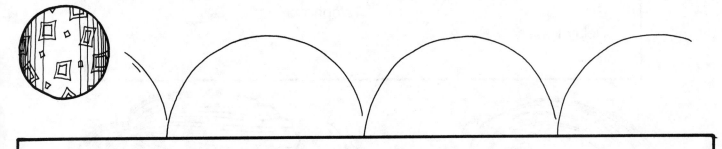

Vary games and activities to include skills of different types. Do not have only relay or physical games; include guessing games or crafts for those not athletically inclined.

If you have a variety of age levels present, do not stimulate competition among guests. Carnival-type games provide youngsters with an opportunity to win prizes without having to compete with one another.

For parties with young children, provide plenty of toys for them to play with when they tire of planned activities.

To burn off excess energy, include a game which involves running and jumping (if you have a backyard or large indoor space).

Do not fill all the party time with games; allow some time for free play, especially in the yard if you have one. This is a real help for the 7—9 age group.

Whatever games and activities are being planned for the party, have two or three more than you think you will have time. Then, if one does not sell, or goes more quickly than expected, you are not left with a bunch of restless kids.

Seasonal Adaptations for Traditional Games

With a few minor changes, many of our favorite childhood games can be adjusted to fit a holiday theme. We have come up with a list of all-time winners and their holiday adaptations. Use your imaginations; add to the games or invent your own holiday fun.

Traditional Games

Tag	Charades
Red Light	Mother May I
Red Rover	Drop the Handkerchief
Musical Chairs	Three-Legged Race
Capture the Flag	Sack Race (jump to finish line with
Pin the Tail on the Donkey	legs inside bag)
Simon Says	Telephone
Relay Races	

ADAPTATIONS:

Pin the Tail on the Donkey easily becomes:

Pin the Star on the Christmas Tree
   Pipe on the Snowman
   Nose on the Clown
   Mouth or Nose on the Pumpkin
   Heart on Raggedy Ann or Andy
   Diploma on the Graduate
   Hat on the Witch
   Nose, Tail, whatever on popular animal or
      character

Use a piece of tape rather than a pin for the young children.
If the traditional blindfolding is frightening to some, suggest they
just close their eyes. Watch for peekers!

For the more ambitious party planner, a more complicated version of Pin the Tail follows.

Pin the Face on the Dummy

Before the Party:
1. Fold a plain twin sheet in half lengthwise
2. With a child lying on the sheet, trace around her body. Add 3'' extra width around all outlines.
3. Cut out.
4. Sew it up leaving 4'' of space in places for stuffing. Also leave one large open area on the side of body for turning inside out.
5. Clip turned seams. Turn right side out.
6. Stuff tightly. We suggest polyester fiberfill.
7. Slip stitch all openings closed.
8. Dress or draw clothes on dummy (optional).
9. Make eyes, nose, mouth, ears from felt or fabric backed with cardboard.
10. **At the party**, guests pin on facial parts with straight pins while blindfolded.

Candy Guessing Game: Decorate any clear jar(s) with seasonal accents: ribbons, stickers, paint, dry flowers, etc. Fill the jar with candy. Be sure to count the candies as you fill the jar. Let the party guests try to guess the number of candies in the jar. The winner keeps the jar.

Valentine's Day—candy hearts
Easter—jellybeans, small chocolate eggs
Halloween—candy corn
Christmas—small candy canes, chocolate kisses

Musical Chairs: This classic favorite can easily be adapted to fit your holiday party. Rather than using chairs, make construction paper cutouts of pumpkins, hearts, trees, Easter eggs, whatever. Place the cutouts in a row (one for each child) or circle as you would for musical chairs and start the music. Remove one ''chair'' at a time as children circle around the row. When music stops, each child must scramble for a chair and sit or stand on it. The one left without a seat is out. Continue until one wins. The game becomes musical pumpkins, musical hearts, whatever your fancy!

Relays: As with musical chairs, a simple adjustment can turn a relay race into a holiday challenge. Assign teams and provide construction paper cutouts, fitting for the holiday occasion, to be passed from one player to another after the lead person has completed running, walking, jumping, whatever relay activity has been assigned. Pumpkins, hearts, Santas, trees, Easter eggs, bunnies—any cutout work may be used.

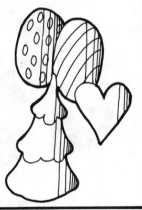

Muffin Tin Toss: Have children toss a specified number of candies into muffin tins from a designated distance. Use candies appropriate to the season.

Easter—jellybeans
Halloween—candy corn
Christmas—silver chocolate kisses
Valentine's Day—candy hearts

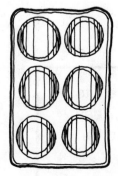

Whoever gets the most candies into the cups in the muffin tins wins. For a prize, award a bag of the candies used for tossing.

Holiday Hunt: From construction paper cut 8 per child of the following:

Orange pumpkins—Halloween
Trees—Christmas
Hearts—Valentine's Day
Shamrocks—St. Patrick's Day
Rabbits—Easter

Hide these shapes inside or out before the party. On your signal, tell the children they are to find as many hidden cutouts as possible before you call time. Provide paper bags for each child to keep the shapes. Whoever finds the most is the winner.

Capture the Flag: Rather than a flag, this outdoor game can be played as Capture the Pumpkin, Capture the Easter Basket, Capture the Christmas Present, Capture the Valentine. Divide the guests into two groups. Each group lines up and places their "flag" at a spot behind their group. On a given signal, children attempt to steal the opponents' flag without being tagged. If they are tagged, they must freeze. Whichever team steals the "flag" and returns to their territory without being tagged wins.

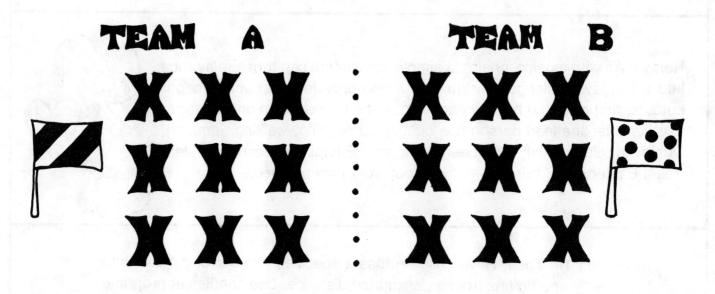

Holiday Word Scramble: Give the children pencils and paper. They are to write down as many short words as they can from the holiday name. Whoever forms the most words is the winner. Christmas: mast, stars, his, hair, etc.

Follow the Leader: This is a good game to play as the party guests are just arriving. Each one can join in as they come. Design a mini obstacle course for the group to follow the leader through.

Red Light: This is a game in which children sneak their way toward "it." "It" turns her back on the players and counts to ten as fast as she can, while the others quickly run toward her. Anyone caught moving when "it" turns around must return to starting point.

Red Rover: Divide the group into two teams. Instruct the teams to stand on opposite sides of the room and hold hands. The first team calls a player from the other team by calling, "Red Rover, Red Rover, send **Amanda** right over." The player called runs across the room to the opposing team and attempts, with one try, to break through their linked arms. If she succeeds, she takes a player back with her to join her team. If she does not break the chain of hands, she must remain on that team.

Simon Says: A person is chosen as the leader. She directs the players to perform certain motions. They may move only if the command is preceded by the phrase "Simon Says." Anyone caught moving without "Simon Says" is eliminated.

Mother May I: This is one of many games in which a group of children make their way toward "it." "It" directs her pursuers to take baby steps, hops, giant steps, whatever. Guests must ask, "Mother May I?" before proceeding, or they get sent back to the beginning.

Drop the Handkerchief: Children form a circle and face the middle. "It" walks around the outside with a handkerchief which she drops in back of someone, who then chases "it" around the circle. If "it" makes it to the empty slot without being tagged, the other child is "it."

I See Something: Sit children in a circle. Start the game by saying, "I see something red. Can you guess what it is?" Go around the circle letting each child make a guess until someone guesses correctly. The winner then becomes the leader.

Sharing Stories: Children sit in a circle on the floor. One child starts telling a story and each successive child must add to it. They can add a word, sentence or phrase, depending on the age group. You may want to set a limit on how long each child may talk.

Telephone: Sit in a circle. You begin play by whispering a sentence into the ear of the child to your right. That child then whispers what she heard to the child on her right. Continue whispering until the sentence has reached around the circle to the last child. She must repeat what she heard aloud. The difference between what was originally said and the final interpretation usually produces gales of laughter.

Hot, Warm, Cold: Have children form a circle. Choose one child to go out of the room or to cover her eyes while another child hides an object so everyone else in the circle sees where the object is hidden. Send for the child to return and tell her what object is hidden. As she searches for the missing piece, children shout out ''cold'' for far away, ''warm'' for approaching the object, and ''hot'' for right near the object. Take turns until each child has had a chance to be it.

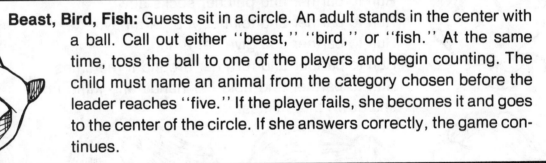

Beast, Bird, Fish: Guests sit in a circle. An adult stands in the center with a ball. Call out either ''beast,'' ''bird,'' or ''fish.'' At the same time, toss the ball to one of the players and begin counting. The child must name an animal from the category chosen before the leader reaches ''five.'' If the player fails, she becomes it and goes to the center of the circle. If she answers correctly, the game continues.

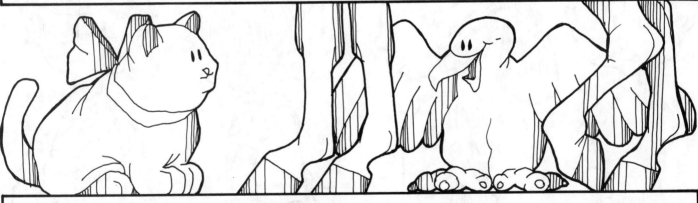

Animals Fly: Have children sit in a circle. Adult starts off as the leader in the center of a circle. When the leader calls out an animal that flies (crow, robin, flying squirrel), children must wave their arms. Child who does not wave her arms is out, or if she waves for an animal that does not fly (elephant), she is also out. This can be adapted to fish who swim, animals that jump, animals that hunt, night animals, etc.

Tell Your Partner: Any number of children may play as long as there is an equal number. Each child picks a partner and then stands opposite the partner with plenty of room in between.

```
Row A- - - - - - - - - - - - - - - - - - -Row B
   1 - - - - - - - - - - - - - - - - - - -1
   2 - - - - - - - - - - - - - - - - - - -2
   3 - - - - - - - - - - - - - - - - - - -3
   4 - - - - - - - - - - - - - - - - - - -4
```

Call out instructions for designated rows to follow: Line A, run to your partner and pat her on the head two times and run back; Line B, run to your partner and untie her shoes and run back.

Samples:

Run to partner and ask her
what she had for lunch.
Run to partner and shake her hand.
Run to partner and pull her socks down.
Run to partner and tell her your birthday.
Run to partner and give her a hug.
Run to partner and turn her around three times.
Run to partner and hold her hands and jump up
and down three times.

There are no winners, but lots of extra energy is happily expended.

CRAFTS

While these projects might entail more time and effort, they are often the most rewarding. Every child loves to show off her own creations. Craft activities are fun and therapeutic for all.

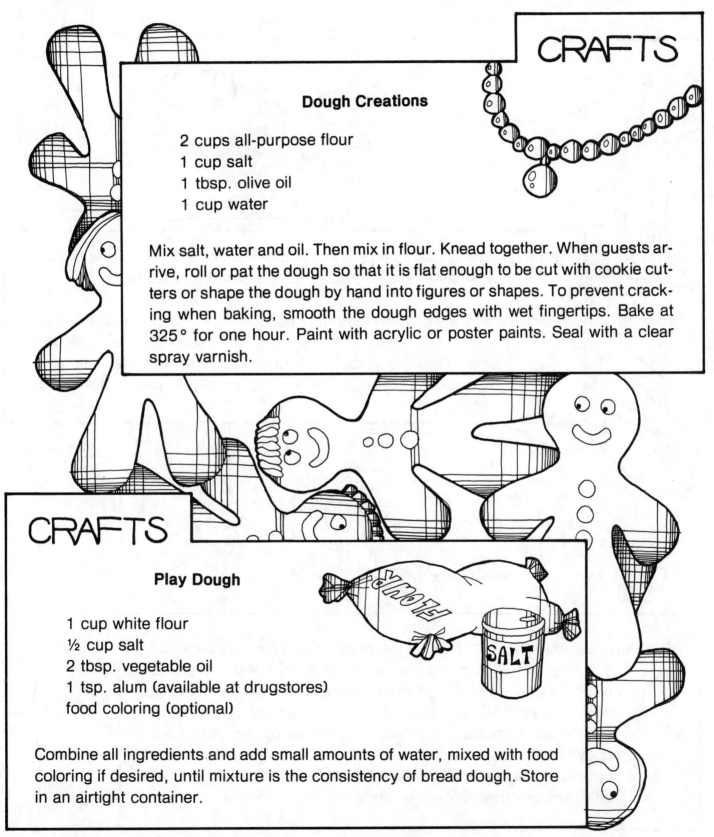

CRAFTS

Dough Creations

2 cups all-purpose flour
1 cup salt
1 tbsp. olive oil
1 cup water

Mix salt, water and oil. Then mix in flour. Knead together. When guests arrive, roll or pat the dough so that it is flat enough to be cut with cookie cutters or shape the dough by hand into figures or shapes. To prevent cracking when baking, smooth the dough edges with wet fingertips. Bake at 325° for one hour. Paint with acrylic or poster paints. Seal with a clear spray varnish.

CRAFTS

Play Dough

1 cup white flour
½ cup salt
2 tbsp. vegetable oil
1 tsp. alum (available at drugstores)
food coloring (optional)

Combine all ingredients and add small amounts of water, mixed with food coloring if desired, until mixture is the consistency of bread dough. Store in an airtight container.

Finger Painting: Mix ¼ cup liquid laundry starch with two drops of food coloring **or** one teaspoon powder paint. You provide the paper; children provide ten eager little fingers. Remember, this is messy and needs ample work space. A variation of this recipe uses instant pudding mix. This edible painting is still messy, but children can clean up as they go!

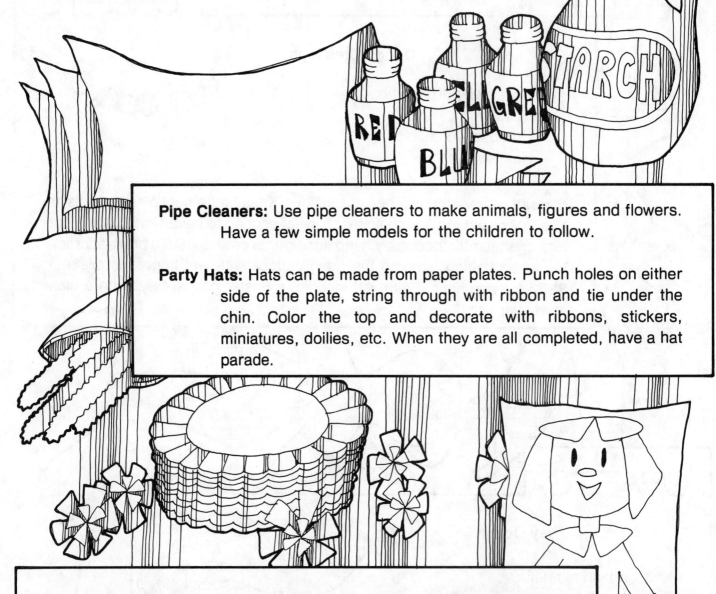

Pipe Cleaners: Use pipe cleaners to make animals, figures and flowers. Have a few simple models for the children to follow.

Party Hats: Hats can be made from paper plates. Punch holes on either side of the plate, string through with ribbon and tie under the chin. Color the top and decorate with ribbons, stickers, miniatures, doilies, etc. When they are all completed, have a hat parade.

Self-Portraits: Materials—(1) butcher paper, at least 30 inches wide and cut in lengths approximately as tall as each guest. (Paper is available from art supply stores or sometimes a local butcher. It may be called poster paper.) (2) wide-tipped colored markers (3) crayons or poster paints. Each child lies on her back on a body-sized piece of butcher paper. Trace around each child, cut out the body shape and distribute the markers, crayons or paints. Let them take their look-alikes home.

Birthday Banner: Materials—(1) butcher paper (2) construction paper (3) crayons (4) scissors (5) rubber cement (6) old greeting cards, magazines, fabric scraps, ribbons, etc. Lay a large piece of butcher paper on the floor. Write "Happy Birthday" across the top and let the children add their own messages, wishes and works of art for the guest of honor. Later it can be hung in the child's room as a memento of the big day.

Rock Painting: Materials—(1) basket of clean rocks of varying sizes and shapes (two or three per guest) (2) set of acrylic paints in jars (3) small paintbrushes. Turn the artists loose and watch the rocks take on a colorful personality. When completed, spray with acrylic spray.

Kazoos: Take a cardboard tube from paper towels or toilet paper and a small piece of waxed paper or Saran Wrap. Stretch the paper over one end of the tube and put a rubber band over it to hold it to the tube. Near the open end, make a small hole with a pencil. Put the tube to the mouth and hum. It's an instant symphony of kazoos!

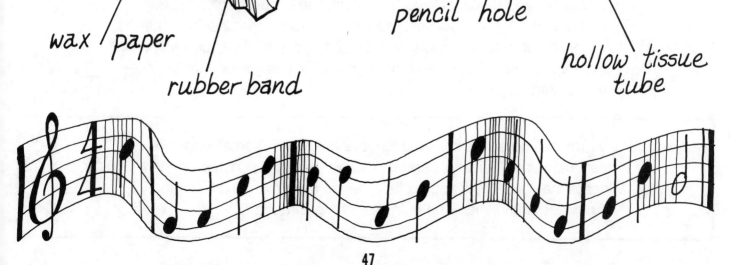

wax paper

rubber band

pencil hole

hollow tissue tube

Guessing Games

Guessing or thinking games make great concluding activities for your party. By gearing the games toward mental rather than physical activity, you will help your energetic guests to "wind down" before going home. Guessing games also provide an opportunity for your less athletic guests to excel and win a prize.

Here are a few guessing games that we think everyone will find challenging.

For the Youngest

I Spy: The chosen leader spies an object in plain view and without pointing to it, announces to the group, "I spy something". . .(names color of object). The guests try to guess the object.

Who's the Leader: One child becomes "it" and leaves the room. The remaining children sit in a circle on the floor. One person is selected to be the leader who will start and change motions that others will imitate. Motions might be tapping knees, patting head, stroking ears, raising arms, etc. "It" returns to the center of the circle to try to discover who is causing the group to change actions. After three guesses, switch "it" and the leader. Tell children not to be obvious in watching the leader. They can peek from the corner of their eyes or even watch a neighbor instead of the leader.

Hot, Warm, Cold: A person is selected to leave the room. A small object is then hidden. When the person returns, the group helps her to locate the object by clapping their hands loudly when the person is near or softly when she is in the wrong direction.

For Older Children

Charades: This is an all-time favorite with children, as well as adults. Each player pantomimes a popular song, book, play or movie. The object is to guess the title.

Word Scramble: Give each child a pencil and paper. Children must scramble the letters of the birthday child's name to form shorter words, for example, Christopher—stop, rope, her, spot, etc. The child who forms the most words in the allotted time is the winner.

Parts of the Body: Guests are given pencils and paper. In a specified time, they must think of ten parts of the body that are spelled with only three letters in each word. This is not as easy as you might think! Answers: gum, lip, ear, eye, arm, leg, hip, rib, jaw, toe.

Memory Game: Bring a tray out with a number of objects on it: thimble, scissors, eraser, magic marker, plate, etc. Let the children look at the tray for three minutes; then remove it. Instruct the guests to write down the objects they remember. Whoever remembers the most items is the winner.

Guess Who: Great for adult parties, too! Prior to the party, write down different names of famous people on small pieces of paper, one per child. Pin or tape a slip to the back of each child (without her knowing what the name is). The children must then ask others questions (which can only be answered with a ''yes'' or ''no'') about their identity, in order to guess who they are.

Camouflage: Before the party, hide small objects around a room, but place them where they can be seen. They are "hidden" by being placed next to something else with the same color. For example, you might put a green leaf against a green curtain, a red thread on the arm of a red upholstered chair, a blue button in a blue ashtray, or a strip of Scotch tape on the base of a lamp. Prepare a list of objects for each child. Be sure to keep a master list of objects for each child. Be sure to keep a master list of where objects are hidden. At the party give list, paper, and pencils to players. When they find the objects, they write down where the items are hidden, but do not disturb them. Allow about ten minutes. The player who finds the most objects wins.

It's in the Bag: You will need one article in each of ten paper bags. They are closed and numbered. The bags are scattered about the room on tables or chairs so that a large number of guests may circulate. At the party, give paper and pencil to each player. She must guess what the bags contain by feeling the bags and writing the items on the paper. Whoever correctly guesses the most items within the time limit (about 15 minutes) is the winner. Some objects you might include are golf ball, sponge, book, pencil, whistle, small stuffed animal or rock.

Test Your Nose: Prior to the party, place in separate bags items which can be identified by odor (cloves, vinegar, garlic, apple, orange, Play-Doh, rubbing alcohol, cinnamon, etc.). Blindfold guests and allow them to guess the items by their smells.

Games of Skill

Games of skill provide a means for healthy competition among children. However, whenever possible award several small prizes for each game, so everyone will go home a winner. For those on the "unathletic side," you might consider prizes for the following categories: tried the hardest, got the wettest/dirtiest, etc., longest legs for jumping, looked most like a deer when running, etc.

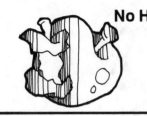

No Hands: String one apple or donut for each child from a tree to a height low enough to bite the apple. Line the children up in front of the apples. The first to finish her apple WITHOUT USING HER HANDS is proclaimed the winner.

Wet Stuff: Great game at an outdoor pool party. Fill a water balloon for every two guests. Knot the end. If the children are old enough, let them fill the balloons themselves. Line up pairs of children equal distance apart. Have them toss the water-filled balloons back and forth. After each toss, say, "Move," and each person moves one step backward away from her partner. A child is eliminated when her balloon bursts. Beware! This is sure to develop into a full-fledged water balloon battle.

Jump the Creek: Place two sticks on the ground parallel to each other about one and a half feet apart. Everyone jumps across. Then you move the sticks wider and wider apart until you have a winner.

Balloon Race: At the start line, children put blown-up balloons between their knees. They must jump to a designated finish line. If the balloon drops or breaks, they must return to start and begin again. Be sure to have two or three balloons blown up for each child.

Variation: If it is a pool party, fill the balloons with water for added excitement.

Obstacle Course: Set up a five to six stunt obstacle course at the co-ordination level of most of the children who will attend the party. Obstacles to consider: throw ball up in the air and catch it; run around specified trees or chairs; take a piece of popcorn from a bowl, throw it in the air and catch it in mouth; jump into and out of a tire; do somersault on the lawn; climb up low stepladder and back down; pour water from one container to another. Position obstacles in a straight line to avoid confusion about what to do next. Start one child at a time. With a stopwatch, kitchen timer or watch with a second hand, time each to see who completes the course fastest.

Hunts

Hunts are a definite favorite with all ages. While scavenger hunts provide a real challenge to an older child, even the youngest party-goer delights in finding peanuts scattered throughout a small area.

A brown lunch sack folded in thirds makes a clever invitation for a party featuring a hunt. At the party, the "invitation" serves as the container for collected items.

Favors can also double as containers for gathered items. Present each guest with a beach pail, basket, plastic watering can or canvas tote.

Peanut Hunt: Hide peanuts (in shells) before the party. The guest who finds the most in the allotted time, wins the prize.

Variation: Hide animal crackers or candies wrapped in clear plastic bags.

Walnut Hunt: Hide walnuts prior to the party. As a highlight, open a few walnuts beforehand, empty and fill with a coin. Glue back together and hide with the others. (Be sure to have some nut crackers handy to check for hidden treasure.) Walnut shells can also be used to hide clues for a treasure hunt. Clues to the hidden treasure are written on small slips of paper and placed in the empty shell. With the guests' combined effort, the clues will eventually lead to the loot.

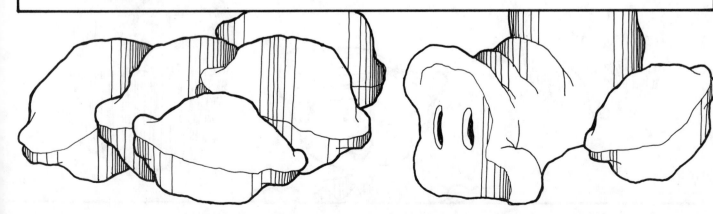

Five-Same-Color Hunt: Before the party begins, cut five squares of the same color from construction paper. There must be a different color (five each) for each guest. Hide the squares around the party room. Ask children to stand in the center of the room. Point out where a couple of squares are hidden. Each child is to pick up one square. She must then find four more of the **same** color to win. She may hold only one color at a time. She may put down all the squares she is holding, choose another color and start again.

Scavenger Hunt: Limited to one area

Before the party, list items to be found; provide one copy per child. Place all items needed around the building. They should be placed in plain sight, no opening closets or drawers, etc. Typical items are: toothbrush, black belt, candle, rubber band, bar of soap, paper clip, sock, ball, doll, etc. Give each guest a list of items and a container. The first to return with all items is the winner.

Outdoor Scavenger Hunt: Children divide into pairs. Give a list of items to each pair. They have 30 minutes to search. Whichever team finds the most items on the list wins. Give each pair two paper cups, two rubber bands, two tissues and a large paper bag for the collectibles. The list of items might include something alive that flies, a cup of dirt or sand, a worm, pinecones, rocks (at least two inches in diameter), leaves, empty can, nuts (acorns, walnuts, pecans, etc.), wildflower, etc.

Spiderweb: A hunt for favors

Each favor is hidden at the end of a long string (colored, if possible) which has been spun throughout your house or outside. Guests wind up the string on colored clothespins to locate their gifts at the other end. This creates quite a tangle, so allow plenty of time for the hunt!

Races and Relay Games

Besides helping to promote team spirit, relay races are terrific for channeling some of that endless energy abounding at every party. Team games also provide the opportunity to award small prizes to most of the guests; this makes each of them feel successful. We think it is worthwhile to include at least two relay races at your party.

Basic Relay: Run, hop, jump, skip to a chair; go around it and back to team member, who is tagged. The process is repeated until each team member has had a turn. The team that finishes first is the winner.

Ball or Beanbag Relay: The first player passes the ball overhead to the player behind. The last person in the team line then passes the ball overhead to the person in front of her. When the ball reaches the first person, she passes it under her legs to the person behind her. The first team to pass the ball to the front person again wins.

Cracker Relay: Each team member races to a designated spot and eats a cracker. Before she can return to tag the next teammate, she must whistle for the ''judge.''

Balloon Relay: Each team member races to a designated spot and sits on a balloon until it pops. Then she returns to her team, tags the next person in line and the process is repeated. Be sure to have plenty of balloons (one per guest) blown up prior to party, and you will need to have someone available during the race to replace each balloon when it is popped.

Balloon Sweep: Each player must sweep a balloon to a designated spot and back to the team. No fair touching the balloon with your hands!

Water Carrying Relay: Give the first person on each team a cupful of water. She walks or runs to the finish line and back. After each team member has done the same, the winner is determined by the one who has the most water in the cup.

Three-Legged Race: Line children in pairs; tie one leg from each child together below the knee. (Use soft rope, old neckties, strips of sheet or fabric.) Send the pairs off toward the goal and back. First pair back is the winner.

Scoop Bean Relay: You will need about one pound of red kidney beans uncooked. Prior to party, count out about fifty beans for each team and put them in small containers. Place full container at teams and empty containers on the finish line. Players are to scoop up as many beans as possible with a teaspoon, run to empty container and fill it. They continue play until you call time (about two minutes). Whichever team has the most beans in their container on the finish line wins.

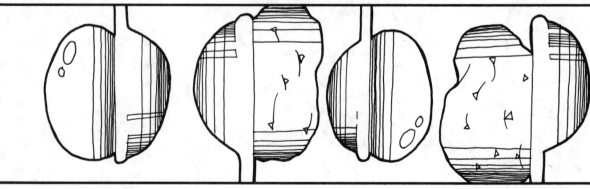

Peanut Push: Each player must push a peanut with a pencil to the finish line and back.

Potato/Egg Race: Each player must carry a potato (or egg) on a tablespoon to the finish line and back. If it drops off the spoon, the player must start over.

THEMATIC BIRTHDAY

"Apples, peaches, pears & plums,
Tell me when your birthday comes."

Teachers, use these suggestions to reward hard work or conclude a unit of study on a particular topic. To create a memorable birthday party, choose a theme which reflects your child's interest and design your party around it. Invitations, decorations, menu and activities should reflect your motif. We have organized complete party plans for you. Thematic birthday plans are presented from start to finish; however, you may want to adapt some of our ideas to suit your particular needs. Thematic parties are easier to plan and create a lasting impression.

While December birthdays do not exactly fit this category, they deserve a few important words. It is easy to get caught up in holiday festivities, but try to make your child's birthday the focus on her special day. If you prefer, and your child agrees, you can have a small family celebration in December, leaving the big bash for a later date. The "un-birthday" or "half-time birthday" celebrated in June seems a popular solution for many December babies. For those who decide to have a party on the actual December date, use a Christmas theme or select another theme outlined in this chapter.

Preschool Crowd

These early milestones should not be very structured affairs. Keep organized activities to a minimum. Do not encourage the element of competition.

Teddy Bear's Picnic

Invitations: Teddy bears cut from brown construction paper with strands of yarn tied around their necks. ''Please Come to a Teddy Bear Picnic for **Katherine**.'' Follow with the party information.

Decorations: Ideally, this should be an outside picnic, so pull out the red checkered tablecloth, inflate the balloons and gather the stuffed bears. Use bear stickers on bibs, place cards, paper cups, etc.

Menu

Bear Sandwiches: Peanut butter and jelly sandwiches cut into bear shapes. (If bear shape is not available, a gingerbread man cookie cutter works well.) Decorate eyes, nose and mouth with raisins.

Jell-O Bears: Combine apple juice and unflavored gelatin; pour into a shallow pan to set. Cut ''bears'' with gingerbread cutters and serve.

Teddy Bear Cake: Body consists of different-sized round cakes covered with chocolate frosting and coconut with gumdrop eyes and nose, licorice rope mouth and toes.

Favors: Choose different calico prints and sew a bear for each child, using the same pattern as the invitation. Stuff bears and tie ribbons around their necks.

Red Party: The idea of this party is to select one color and carry the color scheme throughout all phases of the party. Choose whatever color suits your fancy.

Invitation: Write party details on red paper or red balloon. Instruct guests to appear all in red.

Decorations: Decorate the party room in red from top to bottom: balloons, crepe paper and birthday banner. Do not forget to use red tablecloth, paper plates, cups, napkins and plastic utensils.

MENU

Even some of the edibles should be red: red fruit punch, strawberries, watermelon, tomatoes, jelly or red cinnamon candies. You can also resort to food coloring.

Balloon Party

Invitations: Blow up a balloon, write details of the party with felt markers, deflate and mail in an envelope.

Fold a piece of construction paper in half. Cut a balloon shape keeping a small portion of the fold intact. Glue a short piece of string to the fold. List the party details inside.

Balloon Invitation

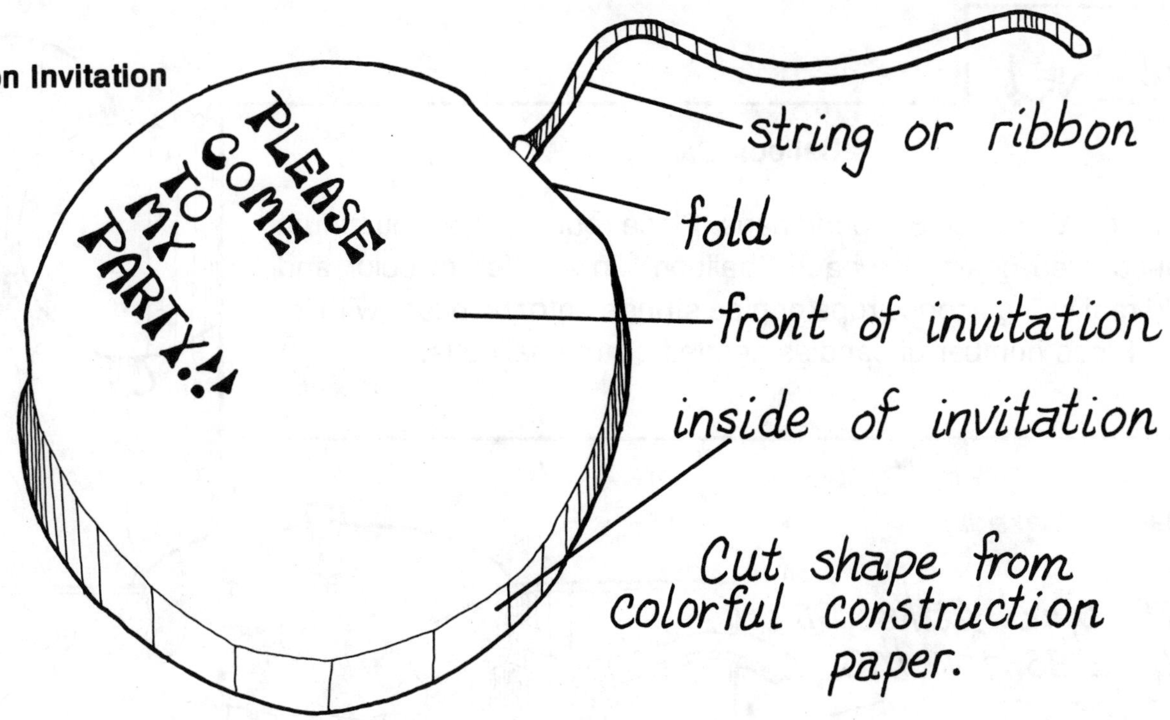

PLEASE COME TO MY PARTY!!

string or ribbon

fold

front of invitation

inside of invitation

Cut shape from colorful construction paper.

Decorations: Balloons everywhere! For a fanciful tablecloth, cut balloon shapes from construction paper. Glue them in bunches on a plain paper tablecloth. Draw string with a black felt marker or glue colored ribbon from each. Display a balloon bouquet as your centerpiece. Write the names of each guest with a felt marker on inflated balloons. Tape a string attached to each balloon to a piece of floral wire (careful not to pop the balloon). Place the end of the wire in styrofoam sitting in a basket.

Balloon Tablecloth

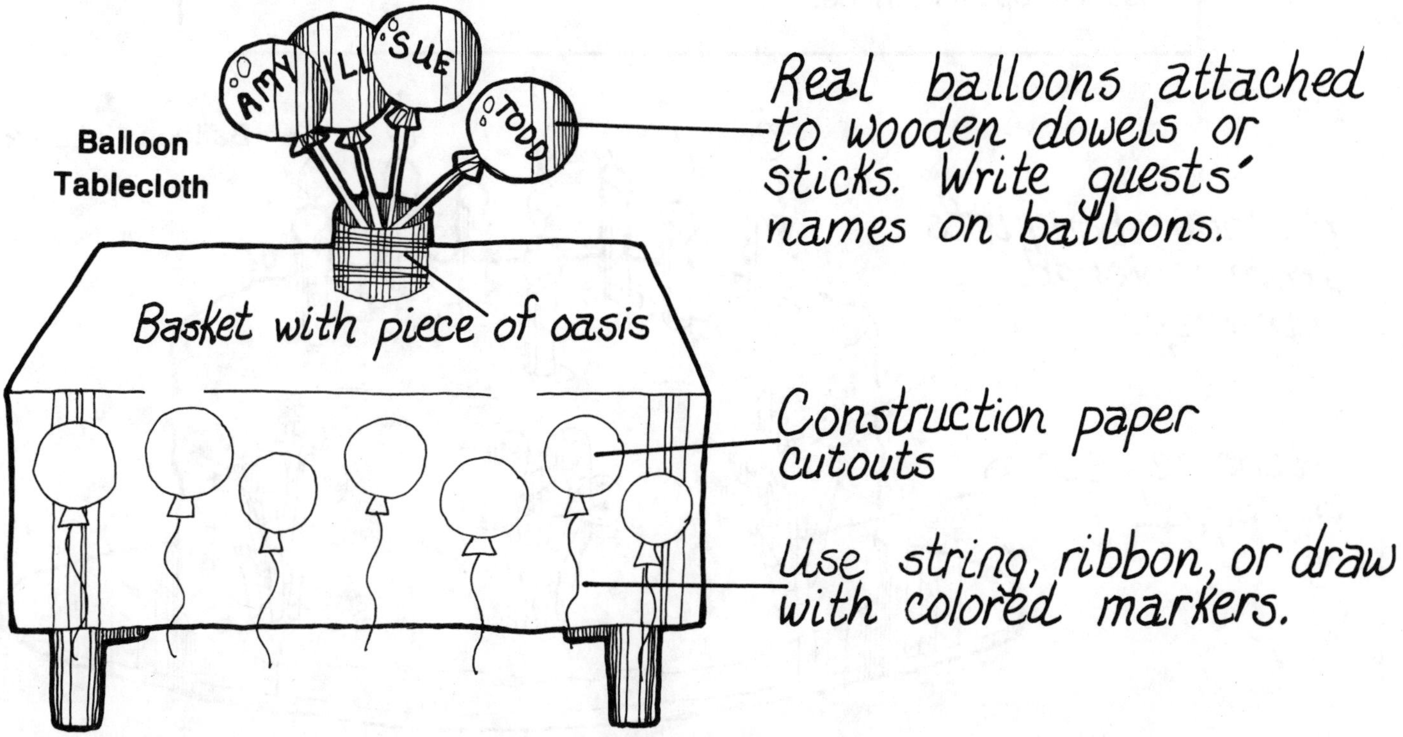

AMY JILL SUE TODD

Real balloons attached to wooden dowels or sticks. Write guests' names on balloons.

Basket with piece of oasis

Construction paper cutouts

Use string, ribbon, or draw with colored markers.

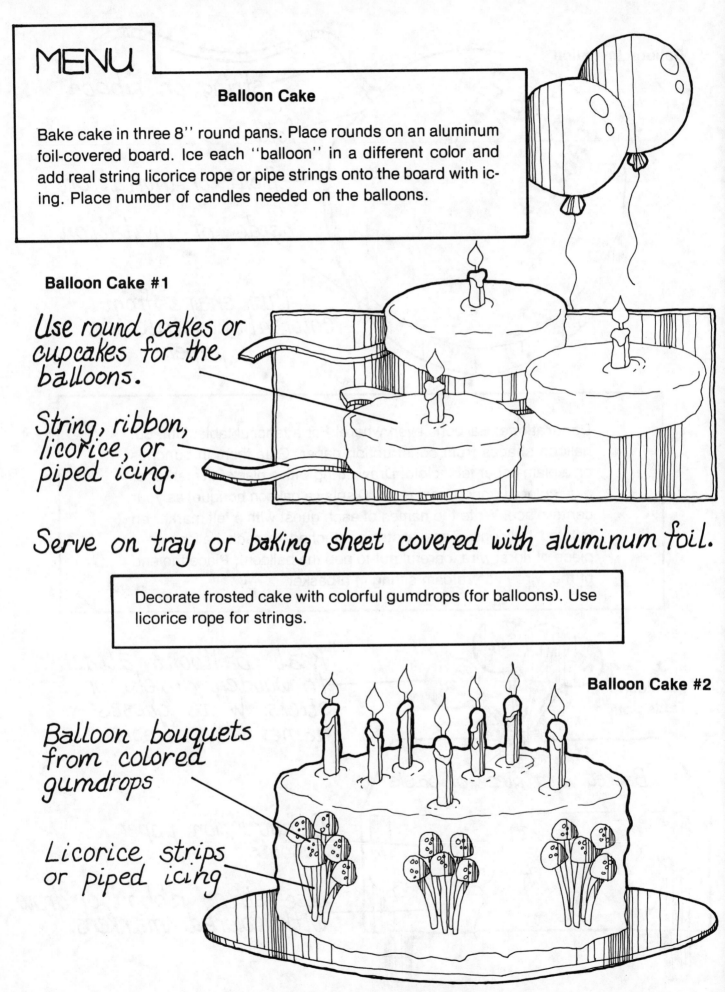

MENU

Balloon Cake

Bake cake in three 8'' round pans. Place rounds on an aluminum foil-covered board. Ice each ''balloon'' in a different color and add real string licorice rope or pipe strings onto the board with icing. Place number of candles needed on the balloons.

Balloon Cake #1

Use round cakes or cupcakes for the balloons.

String, ribbon, licorice, or piped icing.

Serve on tray or baking sheet covered with aluminum foil.

Decorate frosted cake with colorful gumdrops (for balloons). Use licorice rope for strings.

Balloon Cake #2

Balloon bouquets from colored gumdrops

Licorice strips or piped icing

PUDDLE PARTY

Order a warm, sunny day for this splashy affair and bring out your baby pool and water sprinkler.

Invitation: Cut frog shape from green construction paper.

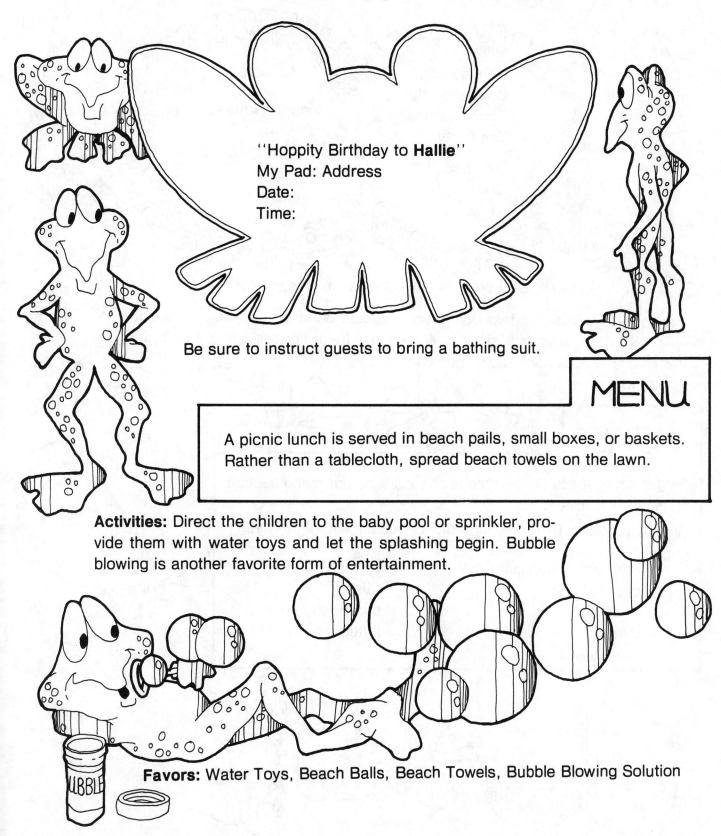

''Hoppity Birthday to **Hallie**''
My Pad: Address
Date:
Time:

Be sure to instruct guests to bring a bathing suit.

MENU

A picnic lunch is served in beach pails, small boxes, or baskets. Rather than a tablecloth, spread beach towels on the lawn.

Activities: Direct the children to the baby pool or sprinkler, provide them with water toys and let the splashing begin. Bubble blowing is another favorite form of entertainment.

Favors: Water Toys, Beach Balls, Beach Towels, Bubble Blowing Solution

FEELING FANCY

For Girls Only

Invitation: Write on a large doily or paper doll cutout:

Bridge Party
Cocktail Party
Formal Dinner
Tea Party

Honoring **Annie Stover**

Address:
Date:
Time:

Dress: Raid your mom's closet and deck yourself out!

Decorations: Decorations should be fancy and frilly. Cover the tables with cloths; candles and fresh flowers add a nice touch. Cut paper doll place cards.

MENU

Finger sandwiches cut into fancy shapes (See our menu section for sandwich fillings.)

Dress-Up Salad (Arrange ingredients as shown on the next page.)

refrigerator croissant roll
pear half
celery
carrots
black olives

cottage cheese
raisins
shredded cheese
lettuce

Girl Dress-Up Salad

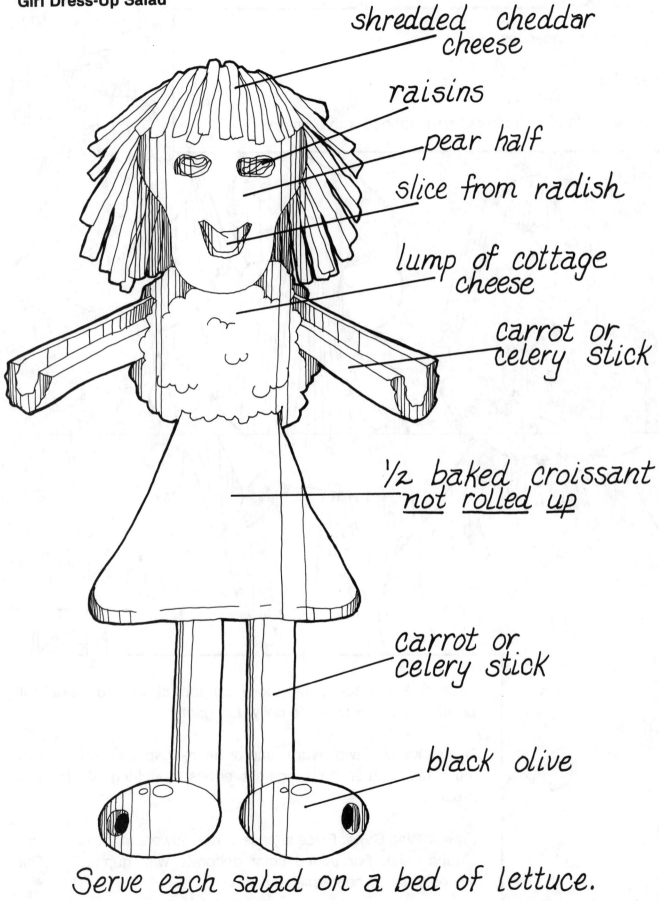

shredded cheddar cheese

raisins

pear half

slice from radish

lump of cottage cheese

carrot or celery stick

½ baked croissant <u>not rolled up</u>

carrot or celery stick

black olive

Serve each salad on a bed of lettuce.

Tea served in teacups

Petit Fours

Ginger ale in plastic wine glasses topped with a cherry

MENU

Lace Cake: Place paper doily on top of frosted cake. Sift powdered sugar over the doily. Lift gently.

Doll Cake: Use two-layer round or heart-shaped cakes. After icing, stand paper dolls against edges, touching all the way around.

Flower Ring Cake: Place a glass of real flowers in the center of a a tube cake. For added color decorate with gumdrops. This makes a dainty centerpiece.

Activities:

Bridge Party: If possible, use card tables. Provide cards to play Crazy Eight, Old Maid, Gin Rummy, Go Fish, etc.

Paper Dolls: Instruct each girl to bring a photo of herself to be used as the face for her paper doll. Cut out paper dolls beforehand. Glue photo of each guest's face to the doll. Provide simple patterns for doll wardrobes. You will need paper, fabric, lace, glue, and all the trimmings.

Fun with Flowers: Purchase fresh flowers, a piece of oasis for each guest and provide inexpensive "vases" (margarine tubs, small ceramic dishes, baskets). Let each girl create a floral arrangement.

Dress-Up Parade: Provide plenty of clothing and accessories: hats, necklaces, shawls, scarfs, dresses, shoes, skirts, and blouses. Turn the ladies loose in the wardrobe room. Add a dab of makeup for the final touch and then the fashion parade begins.

Sparkler: Plan for the "parade" in advance by scouting garage and used clothing sales.

Favors:

Costume Jewelry
Makeup
Bubble Bath
Deck of Cards

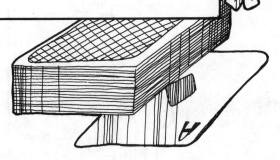

SLUMBER PARTY

This is always a big hit at boarding schools.
Do not lose **your** sleep at the slumber party. Once you have served dinner and supervised games, leave the overnighters to their own devices. If a problem arises, they will seek your assistance.

Invitation: In the corners of your invitation, draw items relating to bedtime: toothbrush, toothpaste, zzz's coming from a sleeping face, bed, slippers, etc.

"Let's Share Some Pillow Talk"
Land of Nod: **Samantha's** house—address
Date:
Time: (Be sure to include time of departure for the following morning.)
BRING YOUR SLEEPING BAG.

Decorations: You will probably want to use traditional birthday decorations surrounding your table. "Un-decorate" the sleeping quarters by moving furniture and breakables aside to allow for sleeping bags.

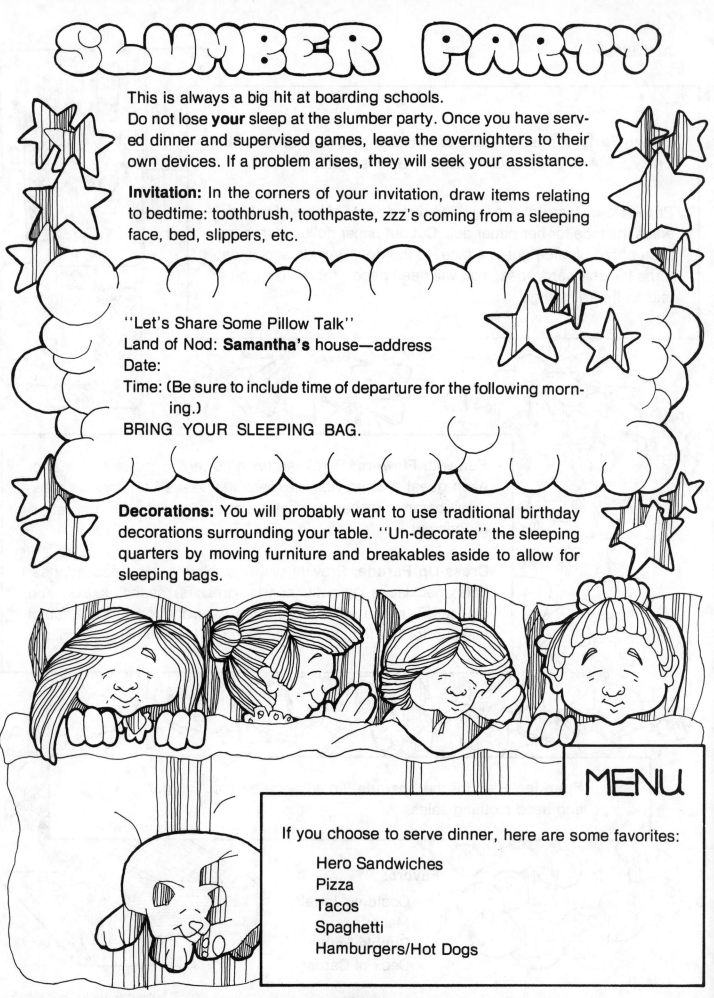

MENU

If you choose to serve dinner, here are some favorites:

Hero Sandwiches
Pizza
Tacos
Spaghetti
Hamburgers/Hot Dogs

Do not forget a midnight refrigerator raid is a highlight of the party. Have plenty of munchies at hand:

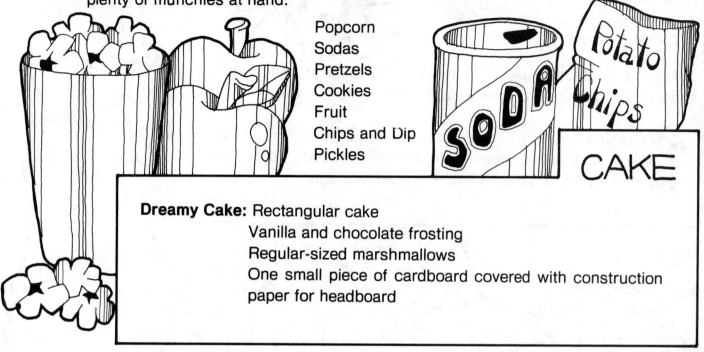

Popcorn
Sodas
Pretzels
Cookies
Fruit
Chips and Dip
Pickles

CAKE

Dreamy Cake: Rectangular cake
Vanilla and chocolate frosting
Regular-sized marshmallows
One small piece of cardboard covered with construction paper for headboard

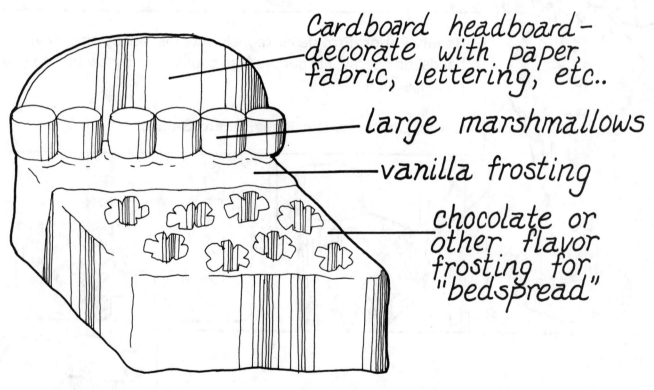

Cardboard headboard—decorate with paper, fabric, lettering, etc..

large marshmallows

vanilla frosting

chocolate or other flavor frosting for "bedspread"

Bake oblong cake for the "bed." Decorate the bedspread with colored icings, flowers, stripes, birthday message, etc..

Do not forget to plan a hearty breakfast!

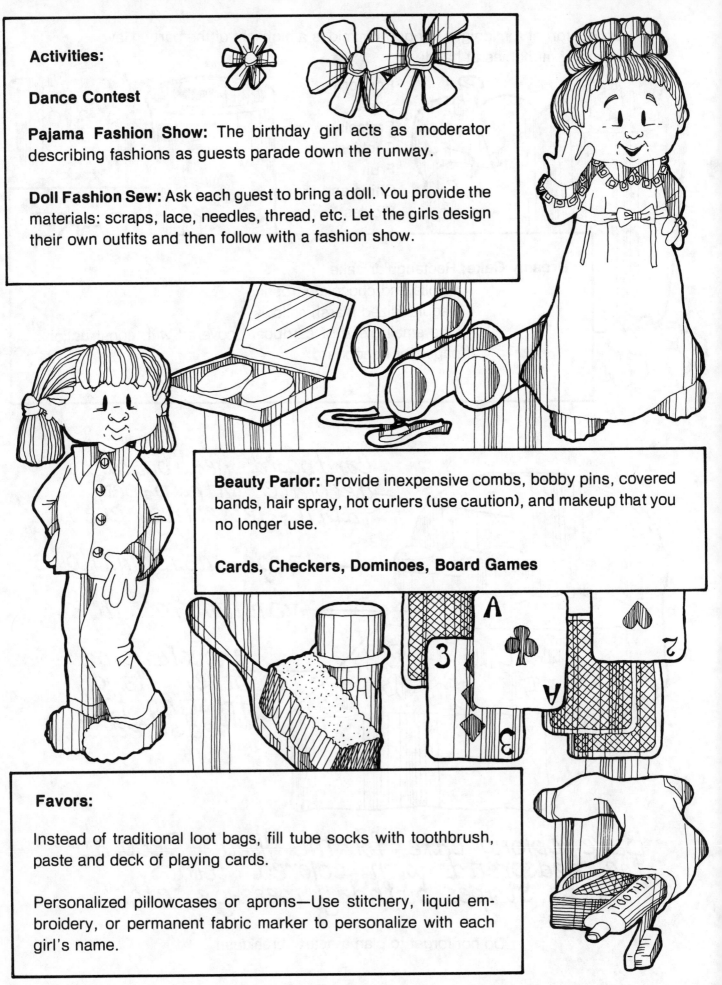

Activities:

Dance Contest

Pajama Fashion Show: The birthday girl acts as moderator describing fashions as guests parade down the runway.

Doll Fashion Sew: Ask each guest to bring a doll. You provide the materials: scraps, lace, needles, thread, etc. Let the girls design their own outfits and then follow with a fashion show.

Beauty Parlor: Provide inexpensive combs, bobby pins, covered bands, hair spray, hot curlers (use caution), and makeup that you no longer use.

Cards, Checkers, Dominoes, Board Games

Favors:

Instead of traditional loot bags, fill tube socks with toothbrush, paste and deck of playing cards.

Personalized pillowcases or aprons—Use stitchery, liquid embroidery, or permanent fabric marker to personalize with each girl's name.

PUPPET PARTY

Invitation: "We will be parading our paper bag puppets at Story's house." Write party details on a lunch-size paper bag. Fold in thirds, seal with a sticker, write address on front and mail. Decorate with a puppet or animal face.

Activities: With a little imagination, lunch-size school bags can be turned into puppets. Instruct the budding artists to create a puppet character. Provide bags, scissors, crayons, markers, yarn (for hair), fabric, lace, etc. Younger groups may need specific character assignments: storybook, TV and cartoon characters. Cut armholes in appropriate places for child's fingers.

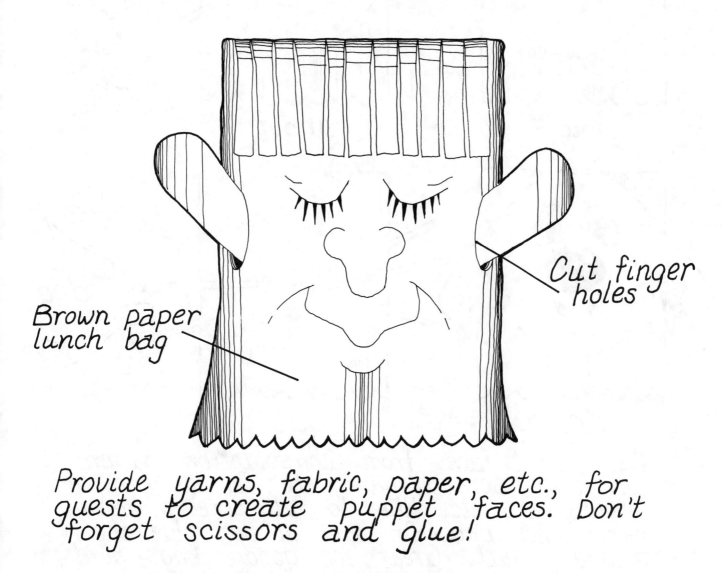

Cut finger holes

Brown paper lunch bag

Provide yarns, fabric, paper, etc., for guests to create puppet faces. Don't forget scissors and glue!

Request a puppet show after the creations are completed.

Favors: Finger Puppets, Small Fairy Tale Book, The Children's Own Homemade Puppets, Barnyard Animals (Barnyard animals made from brown paper bags are terrific loot sacks. This requires construction paper, glue, bags and your artistic talents prior to the party.)

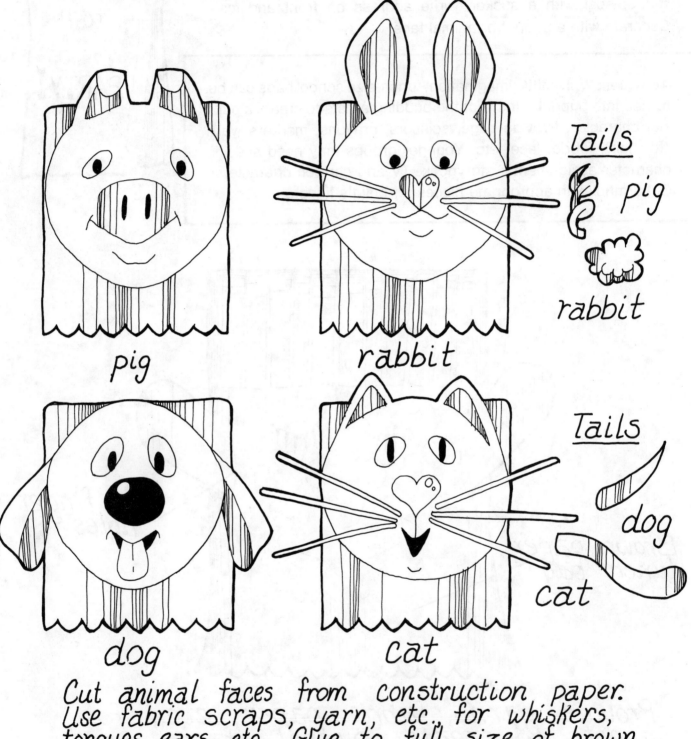

pig

rabbit

Tails

pig

rabbit

dog

cat

Tails

dog

cat

Cut animal faces from construction paper. Use fabric scraps, yarn, etc., for whiskers, tongues, ears, etc. Glue to full size of brown paper lunch bag. On back of bag glue the animal's tail. Great for goodie bags, hunts, or invitations. Create your own animals.

NEIGHBORHOOD PARADE

Invitation: Cut a circular shape to resemble a bicycle wheel. Draw in wheel spokes and write party details around the spokes.

Join Adam's Birthday Motorcade

Include instructions for each child to bring a wheeled toy: wagon, tricycle, doll carriage, bicycle, etc.

Decorations: For this outside party we suggest providing materials for the children to decorate their vehicles: crepe paper, ribbons, empty cans, flags, noisemakers and balloons.

MENU

Paper bag picnics for all

Activities: Map out the parade course with flags, chalk, signs, whatever. Let the parade begin down a quiet street, your property, a park or large parking lot. If the parade cannot be held in the immediate vicinity of your home, specify on the invitations where to meet and be picked up.

Favors: Bike Horns, Sun Visors, Bike Bags, Flags

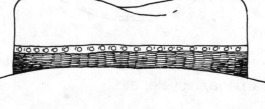

Invitation: We think this one is irresistible. Adapt it to suit your needs.

"Ride'm cowboy to my party"
January 17, 2:30, you'll chow down hearty.
I'm rounding up my friends for some birthday cheer,
At my corral cause I'm turning seven this year.
In Western wear you should be clad,
For the best ole' time you've ever had!

Happy Trails,
Justin

Address envelope as "Wanted: (Name of Guest)."
Use stickers of Western theme on outside of envelope.

Decorations: In a classroom, basement, garage, or on a patio set up a Western saloon. Spread straw on the floor, cover tables with checked tablecloths, cut cactus from green poster board. Prominently display a "Saloon" sign and play country and western music. A bandana makes a great place mat and favor. Place cards made in the shape of sheriffs' badges are cut from yellow paper. In some areas, it is possible to hold a party at a horse farm. In this instance, decorations could be kept to a minimum.

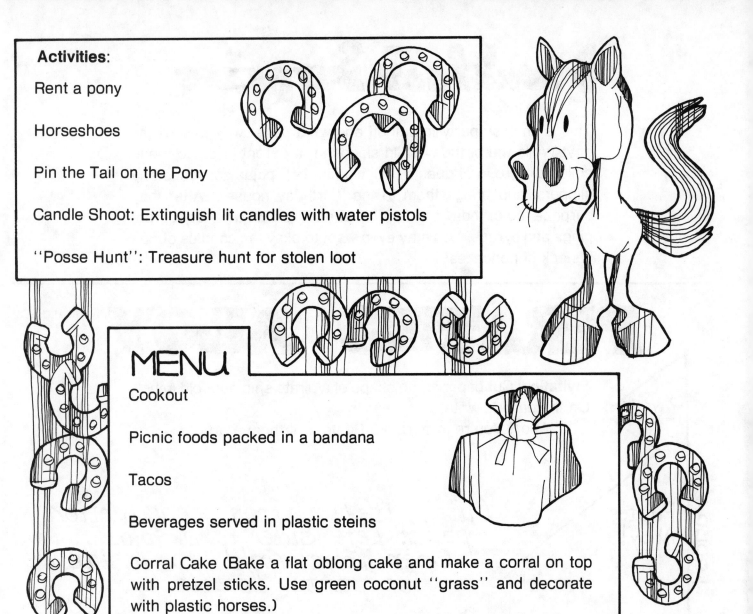

Activities:

Rent a pony

Horseshoes

Pin the Tail on the Pony

Candle Shoot: Extinguish lit candles with water pistols

"Posse Hunt": Treasure hunt for stolen loot

MENU

Cookout

Picnic foods packed in a bandana

Tacos

Beverages served in plastic steins

Corral Cake (Bake a flat oblong cake and make a corral on top with pretzel sticks. Use green coconut "grass" and decorate with plastic horses.)

Pretzel Fence Pattern

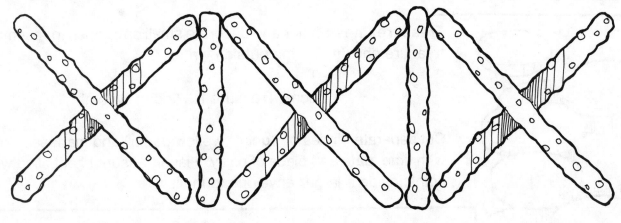

Use thin stick pretzels.

Favors: Bandanas, Sheriff's Badge, Plastic Canteens, Play Money

Breakfast Surprise

This is an easy party to pull off and what better way to start the day! While the birthday child sleeps in, a parent or close friend collects a group of guests (still clad in their pajamas, robes and slippers) and brings them to the "birthday house." After they surprise the birthday child, serve pancakes with a variety of toppings and syrups. You may even want to blow the candles out on a stack of pancakes!

PIRATES AHOY

← FOLD →

Pirates Ahoy!

Invitation: Cut paper in the shape of a pirate ship and fold in half. On the outside write:

"Ahoy! You're Invited to a Pirate's Birthday Party"

Cut invitation from construction paper. Left side is a fold. Open from right to inside for party details.

On the inside include your party details.

Treasure Chest: Color and decorate small envelopes to resemble treasure chests. On the outside write:

"A Secret Treasure Is Hidden Within"

Cut separate circles of "gold" (yellow paper) and mark each one with time, date and place of party. Place treasure chest filled with coins inside a larger envelope to mail.

Decorations: Anything nautical—fishnets, shells, trunk to resemble treasure chest (made from construction paper), swords, eye patches, ship's wheel, parrots, pirate flag over door

Activities:

Treasure Hunt: This hunt takes some preparation, but is well worth the added effort. You will need an empty "treasure chest" with a clue from Teddy the Terrible, who has stolen the treasure. Written clues as well as realistic footprints (made by dipping your hand in flour, pressing down with the side of your fist on the desired surface and adding five dots for the toes) set the hunt in motion. A final clue leads to an "anchor line." Follow the rope to Teddy the Terrible, a stuffed bear decked out with sword, eye patch and bandana. He has all the loot around him—party favors for all.

Simplified Treasure Hunt: Hide foil-covered chocolate candies in the yard. The one who finds the most wins the prize.

Walking the Plank: Place a plank on the floor with a wide pan of water at one end. Choose several "victims" beforehand and jump over the pan of water. While a "victim" is being blindfolded, remove the water. Her efforts to jump the water will bring howls of laughter. One of the spectators may then be chosen to walk the plank. This time LEAVE the water.

MENU

For the ambitious only.

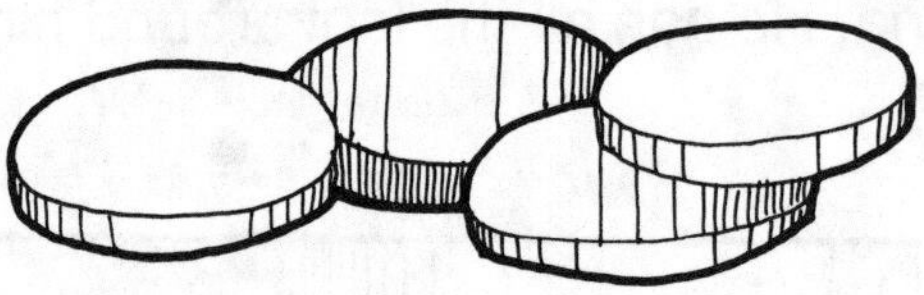

Pirate's Ship Cake

Bake your cake (one that isn't too crumbly) in a 9" x 13" rectangular cake pan. After cake has cooled, cut two boat hulls as shown and then the upper deck.

(13" x 9" cake pan)

Pirate Ship Cake (A)

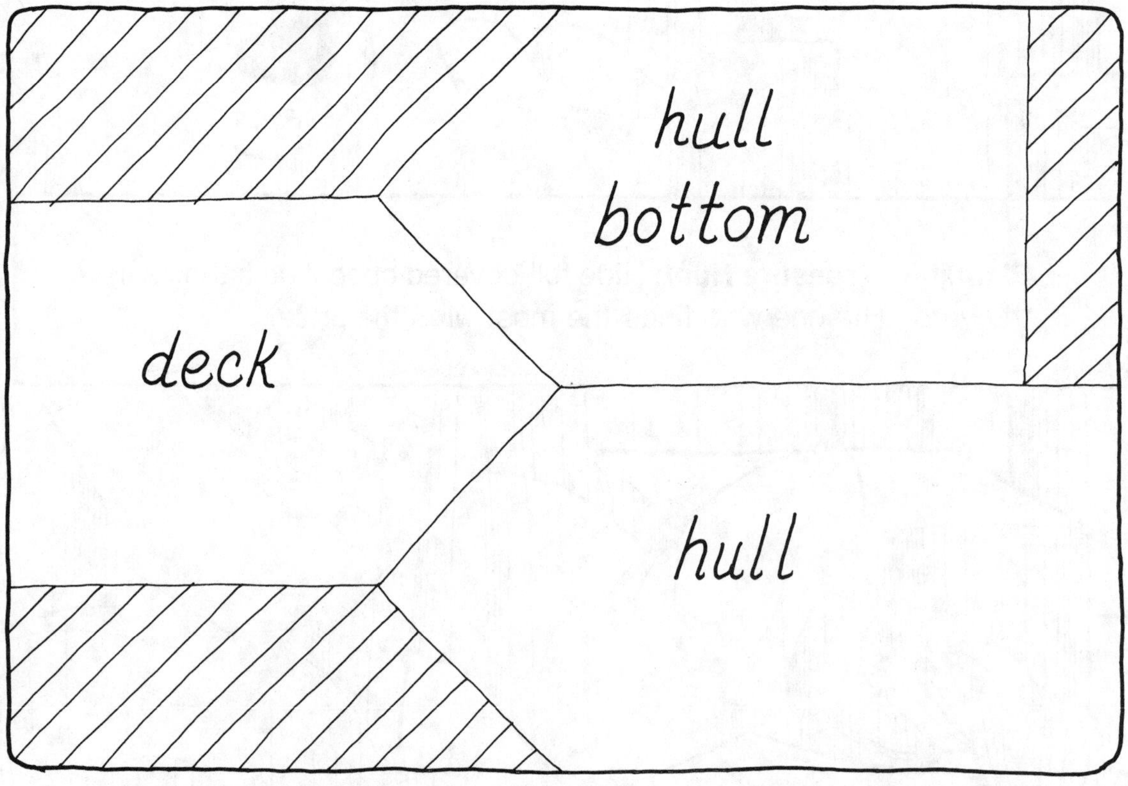

hull
bottom

deck

hull

Layer cake according to diagram on the following page, using plenty of frosting between layers. You may need toothpick supports.

Pirate Ship Cake (B)

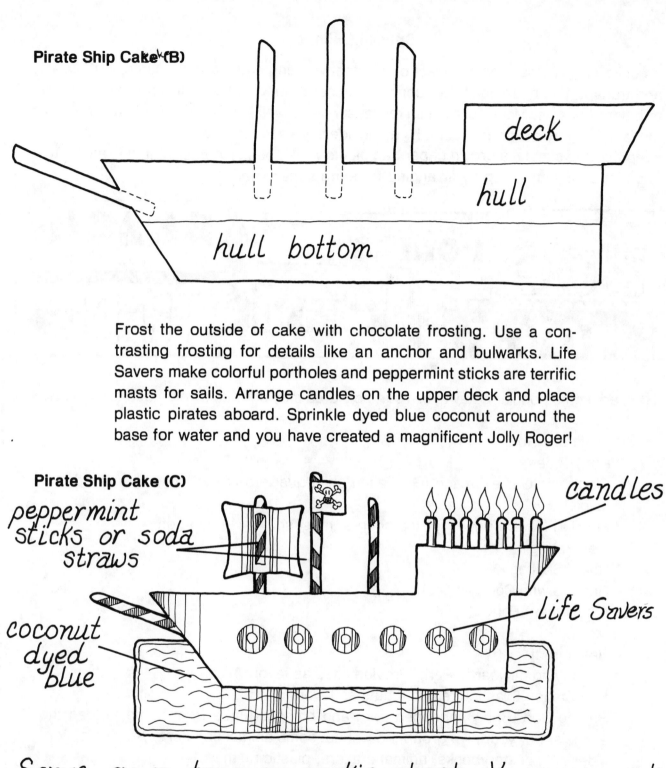

deck

hull

hull bottom

Frost the outside of cake with chocolate frosting. Use a contrasting frosting for details like an anchor and bulwarks. Life Savers make colorful portholes and peppermint sticks are terrific masts for sails. Arrange candles on the upper deck and place plastic pirates aboard. Sprinkle dyed blue coconut around the base for water and you have created a magnificent Jolly Roger!

Pirate Ship Cake (C)

peppermint sticks or soda straws

candles

Life Savers

coconut dyed blue

Serve on a tray or cookie sheet. You may make square paper sails and run them through the "masts"; watch out for the flames from candles.

Favors: Chocolate Coins, Paperback Books of Children's Sea Stories (*Treasure Island*, *China Sea*, *Round the Blue Dolphin*), Bandanas, Pirates' Hats, Plastic Swords

79

Special Outings

As children get older, the prospect of a birthday outing adds to their excitement. Cost and transportation are important considerations; therefore, you will want to limit your number of guests. Make sure to call for reservations well in advance. Find out whether the facility offers a birthday room. If you decide to serve more than cake and ice cream, keep the fare simple; a brown paper bag picnic works best. Another hint: it is easier to keep tabs on your group by arranging for extra supervision.

Here are some popular getaways. Your local area may offer its own unique attractions.

* Miniature Golf
* Pony Rides
* Electronic Game Arcade (Give each child quarters in her loot bag instead of a favor.)
* Bowling (Award prizes for top scores, most spares, strikes, etc.)
* Ice Skating
* Roller Skating
* Hayride with Cookout
* Amusement Park
* Movie
* Restaurant
* Kite Flying at Nearby Park (Provide kites as favors.)
* Fire Station (plastic firemen's hats as favors)
* Petting Zoo (Bring unpopped corn and bread crumbs from home to feed the animals. For your own group, how about some animal crackers? As favors, consider animal storybooks, animal erasers, plastic animals.)
* Dairy
* Train or Bus Ride (engineer caps or bandanas as favors)
* Racketball/Tennis Party
* Beach, Park, or Recreational Area (Your local area may offer its own unique attractions.)

Make your invitation reflect your outing: a ticket for the train ride, animal pictures for a visit to the zoo, hamburger or pizza cutouts for a restaurant, etc.

DETECTIVE PARTY

Invitation: Cut magnifying glass shape from black construction paper. Cut out a circle in the middle for the lens. From white paper cut another circle, write party details on it and glue around circular edge of magnifying glass. Tape clear cellophane over the white paper to resemble glass.

Party Details

White construction paper covered with clear cellophane. Paste white circle on black paper cutout.

Black construction paper

Decorations: Cut or ''chalk'' footprints up to the front door. Hats, pipes, magnifying glasses or any detective disguises can be interspersed throughout the party room.

Activities

Guessing Game: Fill a jar with peanuts, candies, or pennies. Tape the correct number on a piece of paper to bottom of jar. Each guest writes her name and guess on a piece of paper. The winner keeps the jar of goodies.

Seize the Gold: This is based on the popular game Red Light. Place a bag of gold chocolate coins at a designated spot. Line the children up a good distance away and give a signal to start. The object is to be the first to reach the gold, but the children must freeze every time they hear the policeman's whistle. Anyone caught moving a muscle must start again.

Scene of the Crime: This game is a fun group activity. Paste assorted magazine pictures in rows on a large sheet of poster board. Make up a detective story related to the pictures. After the guests study the board, take the board away and question the children about it: "What room was the crime committed in? What color hair did the individuals have? What weapons were used in the crime?"

Treasure Hunts: Locating stolen loot by following previously hidden clues is great fun for little detectives. Details for an elaborate treasure hunt are described for our Pirates' Ahoy Party.

Test Your Detective Skills: Prior to the party, place various small objects on a large tray: pencil, scissors, rock, thimble, eraser, etc. When the detectives are assembled in a room, bring the tray of objects in for inspection. Allow the children to look at the items for several minutes. Remove tray and have the detectives record on paper the objects that they remember. The person who recalls the most objects in the allotted time, wins a prize.

MENU

Magnifying Glass Cake: Make enough batter for a two-layer cake. Pour part of the batter into a meat loaf pan to the depth of one inch. Pour the remaining batter into two round cake pans. After baking, cut the meat loaf shape (for the handle) in half lengthwise. Attach one handle to one cake round. Ice this layer. Repeat this process for the second layer. Pipe a narrow band of chocolate icing around the circle and on the handle.

Favors: Magnifying Glasses, Mystery Paperbacks, Detective Badges, Handcuffs

CIRCUS SPECTACULAR

Invitations: Cut clown faces from construction paper. Write party information with colorful magic markers.

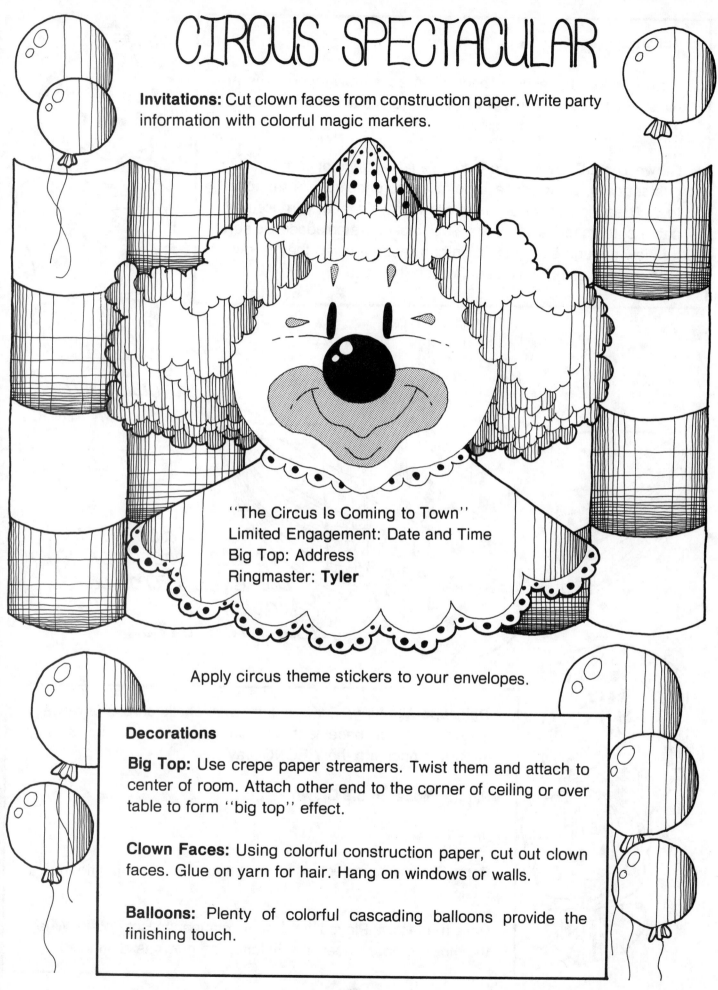

"The Circus Is Coming to Town"
Limited Engagement: Date and Time
Big Top: Address
Ringmaster: **Tyler**

Apply circus theme stickers to your envelopes.

Decorations

Big Top: Use crepe paper streamers. Twist them and attach to center of room. Attach other end to the corner of ceiling or over table to form "big top" effect.

Clown Faces: Using colorful construction paper, cut out clown faces. Glue on yarn for hair. Hang on windows or walls.

Balloons: Plenty of colorful cascading balloons provide the finishing touch.

Activities

Clown Makeup: Decorate each child as a clown when she arrives. Tape a large, white paper collar, folded accordion style, on each child to protect her clothing.

Clown Toss: Draw a clown face on a large piece of cardboard or poster board, cutting out a large hole where the nose is supposed to be. Use markers or paints to draw clown's face, yarn for hair, paper cutouts for hat and ears. Tape clown to stepladder. Be sure it is low enough so the children can reach it when they throw a foam rubber ball or beanbag through the nose.

Cut out large hole for nose.

Cut face from poster board or large piece of cardboard. Paint or color the facial features.

Tightrope Walking: Draw a line with chalk across driveway, garage floor or basement. Performer must walk it, looking through binoculars the WRONG way.

Pin the Nose on the Clown

Ring Toss

Penny Toss: The object is to toss pennies into a muffin tin from a designated distance.

Pass the Clown: Played in the same manner as Hot Potato. When the music stops, whoever is holding the clown is eliminated.

MENU

Big Top Sandwiches: Child-size sandwiches that look like a clown's hat make yummy snacks. Cut peanut butter and jelly sandwiches into triangles. Stick a large marshmallow to the top point of the triangle and decorate the hat with raisins.

Clown Ice Cream: Scoop balls of ice cream and refreeze before decorating. To prevent melting, decorate no more than two balls at a time, leaving remaining balls in the freezer. Place sugar cone on top of the scoop for hat. Use chocolate chips or M & M's for eyes, red cinnamon candy for the nose, licorice lace for the mouth, and miniature marshmallows for collar.

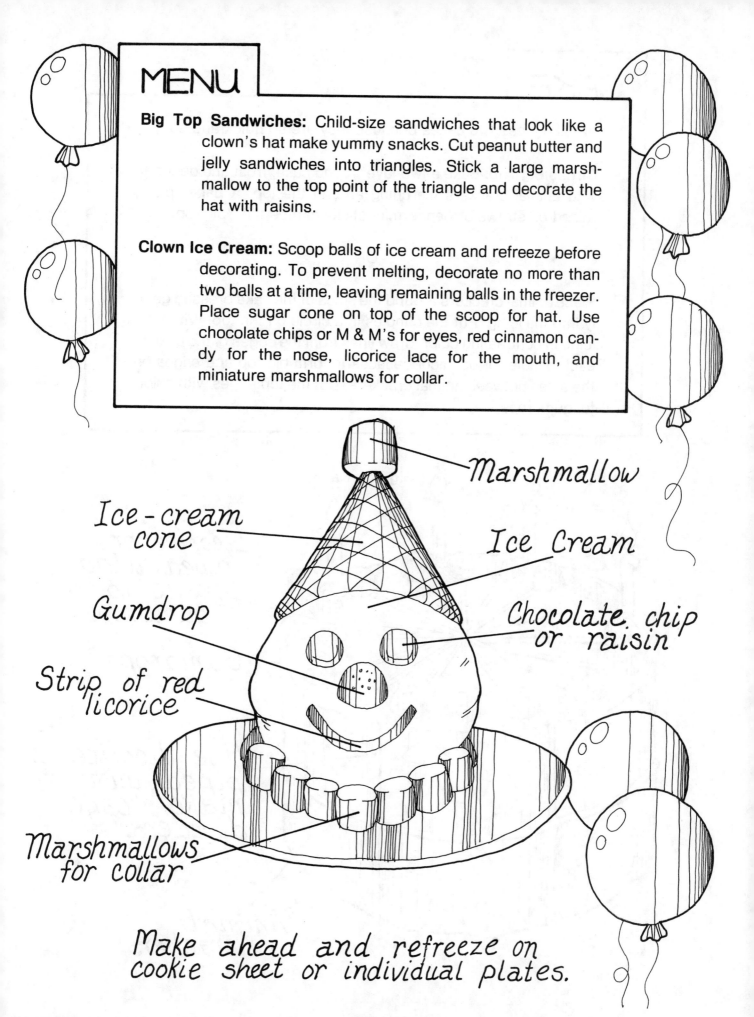

Marshmallow

Ice-cream cone

Ice Cream

Gumdrop

Chocolate chip or raisin

Strip of red licorice

Marshmallows for collar

Make ahead and refreeze on cookie sheet or individual plates.

CAKE

We like these two cakes because they are so quick and easy.

Circus Big Top: Bake a two-layer round cake, frost and decorate with animal crackers marching around the top. A paper plate, raised on straws or peppermint sticks can be the "big top."

OR

Place animal crackers around the sides of the cake pressed gently into the icing. Put the candles in a circle on the top. With tube icing in contrasting color, draw lines from the edges of the cake to each candle, or use licorice laces to form big top and cages on the sides between animal crackers. Dot the top edges with colorful gumdrops.

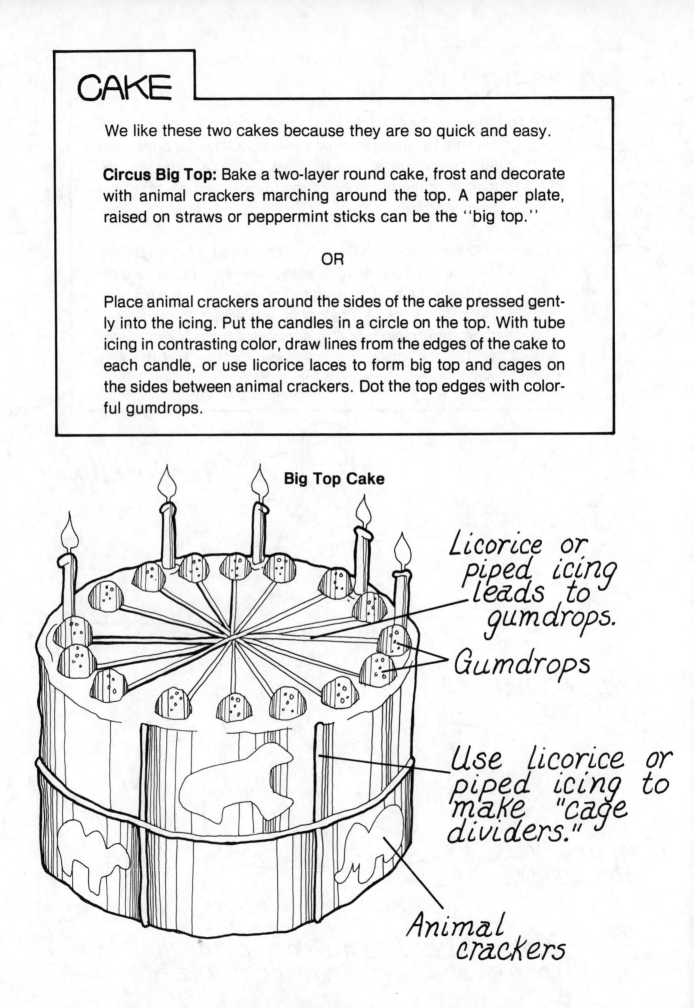

Big Top Cake

Licorice or piped icing leads to gumdrops.

Gumdrops

Use licorice or piped icing to make "cage dividers."

Animal crackers

Clown Face Cake: For the most ambitious, bake your cake in two (2'') round pans. Use one round cake for the face and cut the hat and collar from the second as shown.

Clown Face Cake (A)

Cutting diagram ⟶

Hat

Collar

Use round cake.

On a flat board covered with foil, place the hat at the top of the round cake and collar along bottom. Sprinkle coconut flakes which have been dyed with food coloring on the hat and place a large marshmallow on the point of hat. Licorice laces form eyes and mouth outlines. Red cinnamon candies are placed in the center of the eyes and mouth. Use marshmallows for the nose and along the center of the collar.

Clown Face Cake (B)

marshmallow

dyed coconut

cinnamon candy

licorice strip

marshmallow

round cake

cinnamon candies

Outline mouth with long licorice strip.

marshmallows

Place collar and hat cut from 1ˢᵗ cake round on 2ⁿᵈ cake round to make clown face.

Favors: Animal-Shaped Erasers, Box of Animal Crackers, Paperback Circus Stories, Clown Makeup

PINATA PARTY

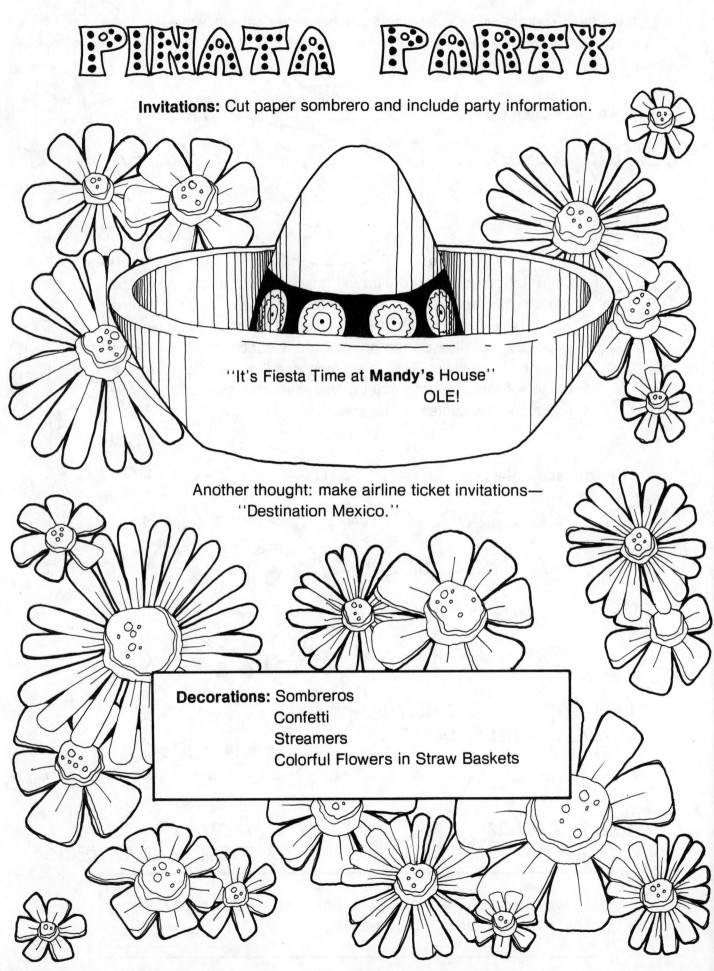

Invitations: Cut paper sombrero and include party information.

"It's Fiesta Time at **Mandy's** House"
OLE!

Another thought: make airline ticket invitations—
"Destination Mexico."

Decorations: Sombreros
Confetti
Streamers
Colorful Flowers in Straw Baskets

Activities: The featured activity has to be the breaking of the piñata. A simple piñata can be made by filling a decorated heavy-duty paper bag with assorted goodies (small trinkets and candies) and tying it securely at the top with a long string. Hang piñata from a tree branch or suitable support. Be sure piñata is low enough for the children to reach with a yardstick or broomstick. Blindfold each child at her turn; then turn her around three times and have her walk to the piñata and beat it in an effort to open it. Each child is given three swings. Once opened, everyone grabs for the loot! The authentic piñata is made by blowing up a large balloon and covering it with the strips of papier mache (newspaper strips dipped in a paste of flour and water), leaving a hole at the top. After it has dried, pop the balloon, decorate the piñata to your liking and fill with assorted goodies. At this point, you must insert a sturdy string and secure to the piñata by sealing the hole with a strip of papier mache or heavy-duty tape.

MENU

Mexican fare is a must. Why not serve ''Make Your Own Tacos.'' Provide tacos and assorted fillings: chopped lettuce, chopped onion, chopped tomatoes, shredded cheese, and ground beef or sausage. Stand back as your guests invent their own concoctions.

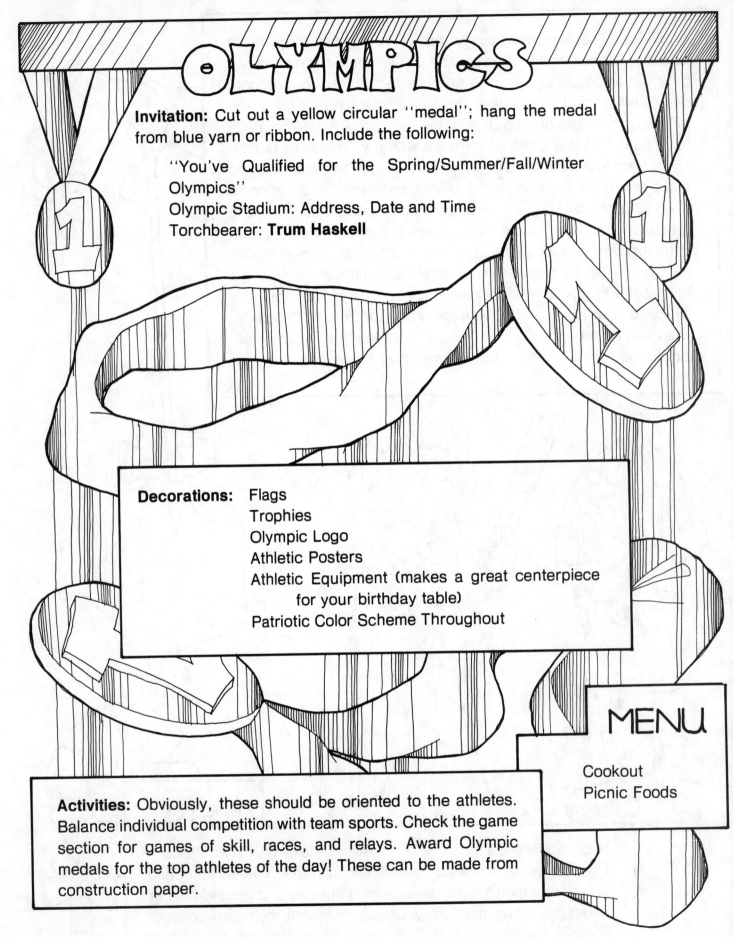

OLYMPICS

Invitation: Cut out a yellow circular ''medal''; hang the medal from blue yarn or ribbon. Include the following:

''You've Qualified for the Spring/Summer/Fall/Winter Olympics''
Olympic Stadium: Address, Date and Time
Torchbearer: **Trum Haskell**

Decorations: Flags
Trophies
Olympic Logo
Athletic Posters
Athletic Equipment (makes a great centerpiece for your birthday table)
Patriotic Color Scheme Throughout

MENU

Cookout
Picnic Foods

Activities: Obviously, these should be oriented to the athletes. Balance individual competition with team sports. Check the game section for games of skill, races, and relays. Award Olympic medals for the top athletes of the day! These can be made from construction paper.

Favors: Inexpensive Trophies, Plastic Sports Equipment

BACKYARD CAMPOUT

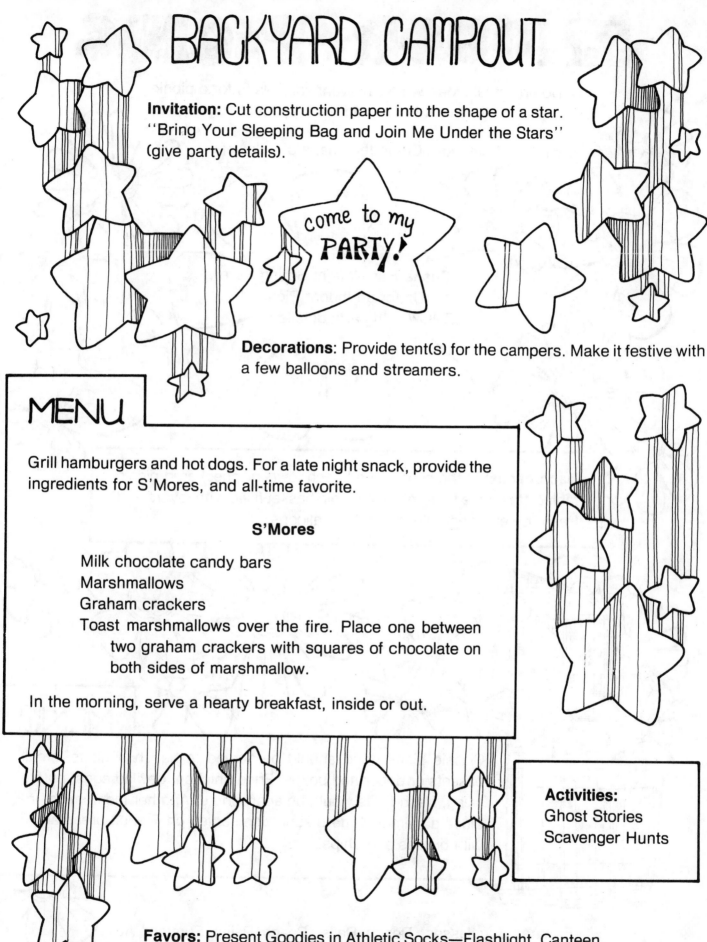

Invitation: Cut construction paper into the shape of a star. ''Bring Your Sleeping Bag and Join Me Under the Stars'' (give party details).

come to my PARTY!

Decorations: Provide tent(s) for the campers. Make it festive with a few balloons and streamers.

MENU

Grill hamburgers and hot dogs. For a late night snack, provide the ingredients for S'Mores, and all-time favorite.

S'Mores

Milk chocolate candy bars
Marshmallows
Graham crackers
Toast marshmallows over the fire. Place one between two graham crackers with squares of chocolate on both sides of marshmallow.

In the morning, serve a hearty breakfast, inside or out.

Activities:
Ghost Stories
Scavenger Hunts

Favors: Present Goodies in Athletic Socks—Flashlight, Canteen, Paperback Book of Ghost Stories, Bandana

INDOOR PicNic

Do not let Old Man Winter prevent your plans for a picnic.
Simply move it inside and think sunny thoughts.

Invitation: Cut in the shape of a flower.

"**Sasha** Has Caught Spring Fever.
Join Us for an Indoor Picnic."
(Follow with party details.)

Decorations: In the center of a beach towel or checkered picnic tablecloth on the floor, place a picnic basket filled with favors and fresh flowers; decorate it with the balloons.

MENU

Classic picnic food should be served in beach buckets, small baskets or decorated boxes. Fried chicken, deviled eggs, potato salad, fresh fruits would be appropriate. Another menu might include a mammoth hero sandwich served on French bread along with pickles and chips.

Favors: Sunglasses, Beach Balls, Beach Pails, Summer Accessories

Let's Go to the Movies

Invitation: Make your invitation to resemble a movie ticket.

ADMIT 1

"Admit One to a Party Premiere"
Theatre: **Katie Kelly's** House
Curtain Rises: Date and Time (ideally this should be an evening affair)

Decorations: Set up a room to resemble a movie theatre. Place chairs in rows, tape a white sheet to a wall for the screen, and set up a refreshment stand to serve bags of popcorn or Cracker Jacks, sodas, and candy. Some theatres will provide old movie posters which would make your home setting more authentic.

chocolate

Activities: Local libraries will often lend children's films. Camera stores will rent projectors, screens, and sound systems. Make sure to reserve a film well in advance. Dim the lights and roll 'em.

Favors: Try to tie in the favors with the theme of your movie. Or you might want to provide each child with a coupon redeemable at a local movie theatre.

MAKE A MOVIE

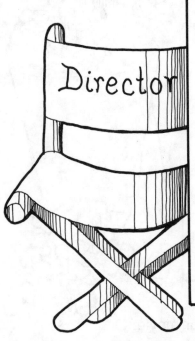

Invitations: Cut star shapes from construction paper.

"We Want You to Star in **Jamie's** Birthday"
Filming Studio: Address
Audition: Date and Time

Decorations: If you are artistic you might design a simple movie set by painting a scene on a large piece of butcher paper or let Mother Nature be your backdrop. Design a sign for your front door: "**Jamie's** Theatre Productions."

MENU

Popcorn
Cracker Jacks
Soda
Candy
Cake and Ice Cream

Director

Activities: When the young actors arrive, assign each a role from a popular story such as *Snow White, Peter Pan*, etc. Provide simple costumes and accessories. If you do not mind the mess, add a touch of theatrical makeup to the stars. After donning costumes and holding a brief rehearsal, the filming begins with your movie camera. A home video cassette recorder provides an instant showing. Otherwise, you might want to invite the actors back for an informal viewing.

A less complicated idea is to film a commercial. Provide products with numbers on the back. Each child draws a number out of a box that indicates which product she will advertise. Set a time limit for each performance. After writing their commercials, the children perform in front of the movie camera.

Favors: Coupons Redeemable at a Local Movie Theatre, Makeup Kits or Disguises

Tacky Party

Bad taste reigns supreme at this affair!

Invitation: On a crumpled piece of scratch paper, write your party invitation.

> "For this affair, don't dress with a flair;
> Your tackiest clothes, we want you to wear."
>
> (Follow with the party specifics.)

Decorations: Use household throw-away items strung up with crepe paper (tin cans, food boxes, detergent boxes, cleaning equipment, old shoes, etc.). For a truly tasteless centerpiece, try dead flowers in a tin can.

Menu: Plan a nice menu, but serve your food on a hodgepodge of tableware; make sure nothing matches!

Activities
Fashion Show: Stage a tacky fashion contest. Designate a master of ceremonies to describe the parade of poor taste—in this case, the worst three win.
Bubble Gum Contest: (1) biggest bubble wins; (2) most pieces of gum in the mouth wins this one.
Dry Whistle Contest: Each guest eats several saltine crackers. The first one able to whistle wins.

SPACE EXTRAVAGANZA

Invitation: Make a construction paper cutout of a star, moon, or rocket ship. Decorate the invitation with gummed stars and glitter.

''Come to a Party That Will Be out of This World''

Astronaut: **Christopher Woodman**

Blast Off: Date and Time

Destination: Address

Decorations:

Poster board cutouts of stars and planets covered in foil and suspended from walls and ceiling

Blue and grey crepe paper streamers

Blinking lights

Silver moons (Wrap styrofoam balls with foil and hang from ceiling with fishing line.)

White and blue balloons

''Black'' lighting

MENU

Space Burgers

Prepare an open-face hamburger or cheeseburger. Garnish with pickle slices, cherry tomatoes, cheese cubes held in place with colored toothpicks.

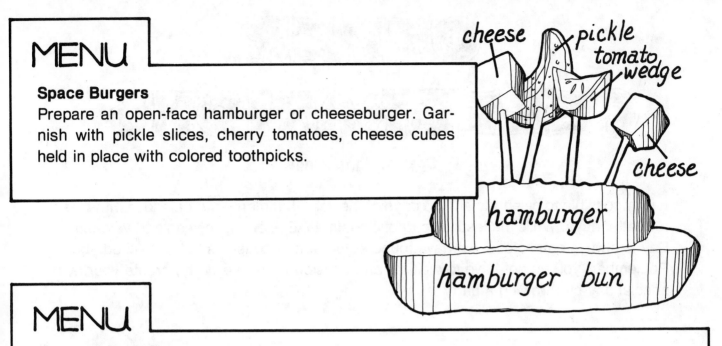

cheese

pickle

tomato wedge

cheese

hamburger

hamburger bun

MENU

Rocket Salad

Cut a banana in half and stand upright on a plate. Surround it with grated cheddar cheese and top with a cherry.

Moonballs

Mix ½ cup peanut butter, a bit of honey and 3½ tbsp. of dried milk together. Roll in granola.

"Marshian" Cake

Position marshmallows to form people across top of sheet cake. Use half marshmallows for arms and legs. With tube icing, dot eyes, nose and mouth. Simple arcs mark the feet and hands.

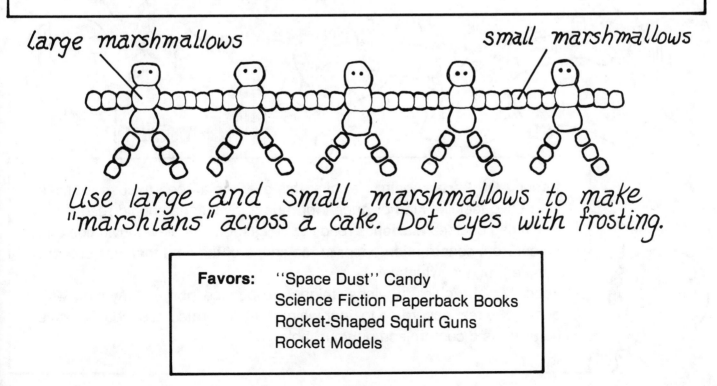

large marshmallows

small marshmallows

Use large and small marshmallows to make "marshians" across a cake. Dot eyes with frosting.

Favors:	"Space Dust" Candy
	Science Fiction Paperback Books
	Rocket-Shaped Squirt Guns
	Rocket Models

OTHER CELEBRATIONS

Special Happenings

It is impossible to celebrate all 365 days of the year, but mark your calendar with these red-letter days. While the festive spirit of Christmas, Easter, Halloween and Valentine's Day is always contagious, we have found some other occasions to get excited about. Remember, you do not have to wait for an occasion to have a party; create your own special day by throwing a party.

Braces Off: Stage a surprise celebration around this momentous event. Phone invitations beforehand, or write them on photocopies of the orthodontist's letterhead. Snacks or dessert are all you need. Simple, but sticky, fare is a must! Include all these taboos: bubble gum, corn on the cob, apples, taffy, peanut butter, etc.

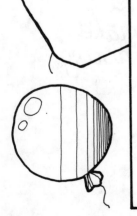

Casting Off Party: Again, we think this event is a good excuse to make your child feel like king or queen for a day. Invitations should read, ''Dr. Smith had decided **Marion** is ready to be cast off.'' A clever invitation can be cut from construction paper in the shape of the limb that was broken: arm, leg, finger, whatever.
Food: May be chicken wings, thighs, barbecued ribs, or anything with bones; the rest according to your whim. The decorated cast could always be used as a centerpiece on your table!

Moving Away Party: Make the transition to a new state or town more pleasant, and provide your child with lasting memories of his old home. Invitations can be made from maps, photocopies of airline tickets, baggage tags, or pictures of moving vans. A bit of nostalgia should decorate the party room. We suggest posters or pictures of the present surroundings: school, church, favorite shops or parks, even photos of friends. Serve the child's favorite meal, and if you are really ambitious, present her with an album of pictures, poems, and drawings done by friends and relatives.

Sparkler: A trip to the library to borrow books about moving may make the adjustment a lot easier. Some moving companies have pamphlets which provide tips for moving with children.

Neighborhood Pet Parade: A spontaneous bash to take the blah's out of a summer day. Invite the children to bring their pets for a parade. An awards ceremony adds to the fun. Make sure each pet gets proper recognition. Award categories might include the longest tail, best behaved, loudest bark, most human, and so forth. Judges can be picked from among the group, either adults or children without pets. We suggest extra supervision if you take on this party!

Sparkler: Make sure children bring pets that will be compatible.

Graduation from Kindergarten or Any Special Class: Anybody at any age loves extra recognition. Signal a major accomplishment by mailing party invitations resembling diplomas (rolled and mailed in tubes) or cut graduation caps from construction paper and attach tassels. Serve sandwiches cut into shapes or numbers. Ginger ale "champagne" can be served in plastic champagne glasses and garnished with a cherry or strawberry. For an activity, try to pin the diploma in the graduate's hand.

End-of-School-Year Party: Another milestone in a child's year is the end of school. Celebrate with family and friends in an informal way. A barbeque or picnic is easiest. Have everyone bring part of the meal, assign a cleanup committee and let the party begin! Games and menu ideas can be drawn from those individual sections of *Parties for Home and School*.

Home from the Hospital: While you probably want to keep this a low-keyed event, a few special touches can make for a happy day. If diet permits, plan your child's favorite meal. For a bedridden child, decorate a bed tray with balloons, crepe paper and ribbons. Have family and friends contribute their artistic expertise by making a welcome-home banner and pictures to adorn the walls of the child's room.

Hot Summer's Day Party: A forever-blowing-bubbles party is a favorite on a hot summer's day. Invite the guests to bring their bathing suits and then turn on the sprinkler. Provide bottles of bubbles (you can make your own bubble mix with liquid soap or baby shampoo and a little water). Wands can be made from pipe cleaners. Serve Popsicles or watermelon ice cream, a taste treat and a visual sensation!

May Day Celebration: Make the arrival of spring official with a grand May 1st celebration. Invitations should suggest the season—a flower cannot miss. Cut the design from construction paper and on the outside include a poem about spring or flowers. Party details should be written on the inside or back. Colorful crepe paper streamers, ribbons and paper or freshly cut flowers brighten the party environs. Maypole dancing is customary. Hand each child a streamer that has one end attached around the maypole. (Pole suggestions: flagpole, tetherball pole—have local lumberyard cut poles.) Turn on music and let the children weave around the pole, wrapping it with the streamers.

Ethnic Holiday: The traditions of these international holidays are passed on from generation to generation. Whether it is the Chinese New Year, St. Patrick's Day or the example we received from Alaska, Norwegian Independence Day, these occasions are highlights of the year. Costumes are a must for these festivities which include athletic competition, parading, dancing, eating, storytelling and dramatics. For the Norwegian holiday, activities include rowing races and folk dancing. Participants are instructed on the rudiments of the schottische and the polka. Of course, the fare needs to be reminiscent of the country, in this case, highlighted by Scandinavian cookies (krumkake, sanbakles, tetkaker, lefse, etc.). Check a library for details on ethnic holidays and consult cookbooks for special recipes. The added effort to make the affair as authentic as possible will make these traditions an important part of your child's life.

Mother's Day: This party was suggested by a teacher whose students helped plan this special recognition for their Moms. Invitations may be cut from colored construction paper in the shape of flowers. A special poem to Mom could be written on the inside.

Decorations should be suggestive of spring; freshly cut flowers surrounding the featured punch make it festive. A tablecloth decorated with construction paper flowers made by the children gives a seasonal focus to the setting.

The punch could be ginger ale combined with Hi-C fruit drink. Float scoops of lime sherbet on top. Children might demonstrate their culinary expertise by bringing in homemade cookies.

Since Mom is the center of attention, activities should include songs, skits, or poems presented in her honor. Give her a real or paper flower as a special favor.

There is no reason why Dads cannot have their day, too. Adjust your plans for a Father's Day celebration.

Arrival of a New Baby

We cannot overlook the importance of a new arrival. A few personal touches will make this day extra special for the proud parents.

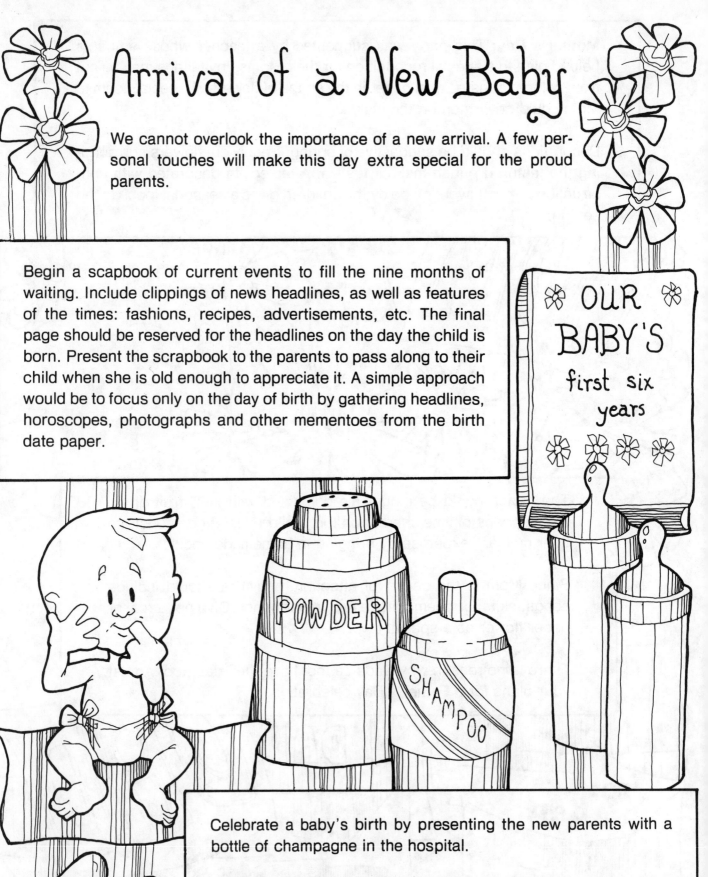

Begin a scrapbook of current events to fill the nine months of waiting. Include clippings of news headlines, as well as features of the times: fashions, recipes, advertisements, etc. The final page should be reserved for the headlines on the day the child is born. Present the scrapbook to the parents to pass along to their child when she is old enough to appreciate it. A simple approach would be to focus only on the day of birth by gathering headlines, horoscopes, photographs and other mementoes from the birth date paper.

Celebrate a baby's birth by presenting the new parents with a bottle of champagne in the hospital.

A favorite way to announce the arrival of a baby is to decorate the mailbox, front door, lamppost, even the top of a flagpole with pink or blue ribbons. For the flamboyant folks, florists will make a huge bow.

Another way to offer congratulations is to personalize an inexpensive wine carafe. ''Congratulations'' could be painted prominently across it. For the ambitious artist, paint the family's or baby's name, a stork, or teddy bear, etc. Use permanent paints that are designed for use on glass.

Welcome the family home with flowers. Why not present a bouquet placed in a baby bottle or the wine carafe described above.

A real labor of love is to prepare the welcome-home dinner. With the help of one or two close friends, this can become a memorable feast. They can put their talents to work and create a gourmet fare.

A picnic basket or cardboard box decorated with balloons, ribbons, and crepe paper is delivered to the parents' doorstep. A menu attached to the outside announces the evening meal.

Tyler's Arrival Home - March 11, 1980

Little Boy Tomato and Burpless Cucumber Salad

Poppy and Mommy Seed Chicken

Baby Early Peas - Better known as Baby
Five Days Late Peas

Good Strain and Mild (we hope) Rice

Pecan Pie Squares - 'Cause everyone wants
to "peek in" at Tyler

In addition to the food, candles, wine and even personalized cloth napkins may be included. Everything is done in blue or pink.

It is easy to personalize cloth napkins by using plastic stencil forms and permanent fabric markers. They add a clever touch to many important celebrations (anniversaries, birthdays, graduations, etc.), and help preserve the memory of the occasion.

Stenciled Napkins

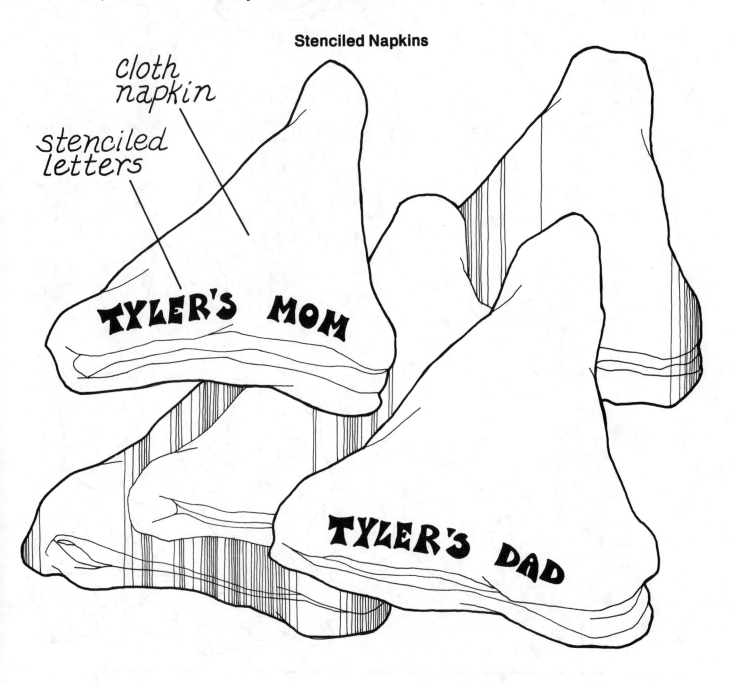

cloth
napkin

stenciled
letters

TYLER'S MOM

TYLER'S DAD

Use cloth napkins and permanent fabric markers. Plastic or paper stencils are best for layout of letters.

As a living celebration, plant a flowering tree to commemorate a baby's birth. This is still possible for a winter baby. Present the parents with a gift certificate with a local nursery to be redeemed during the planting season. Tradition suggests an apple tree for a boy and a pear tree for a girl. Be a real pal and bring your shovel along, too!

Sparkler: When presenting a gift to a new baby, bring a small remembrance to the older children. An easy favorite is to stencil a T-shirt using a permanent fabric marker—''I'm the Big Brother/Sister.''

CHRISTMAS

Make Christmas and other holidays throughout the year more meaningful. Christmas should be more than gift giving, Thanksgiving more than a feast. Include your children in holiday festivities, such as baking and decorating. They will begin to feel an important part of the holiday preparation.

The excitement of Christmas morning can be overwhelming. The anticipation of Santa's surprises, coupled with parents' hopes for their child's delight, can lead to frustration. It may be the candy cane in the stocking which is the hit of the day. Here are some suggestions to keep everything on a happy note.

Help younger children prepare for holiday excitement by reading books about the occasion. Local libraries and churches are good sources.

Advent calendars are fun and a good way to put the often-asked question of "How many days until Christmas?" into perspective.

Place special labels on presents for the nonreader so she can find her presents under the tree. Red circles cut from construction paper, Santa faces, commercial stickers—all work great.

Be patient. Allow plenty of time for unwrapping gifts, especially with a young child. Rushing the process tends to overwhelm a child. If necessary, consider leaving some unopened gifts until later.

Keep some special gifts unwrapped under the tree. This increases the thrill of Santa's late-night visit.

Be sure to have batteries on hand for mechanical toys.

Minimize the commercial aspect of Christmas by having students or family members exchange an ''original'' gift. This could take any form they choose: a poem, story, picture, or collage.

For large groups consider drawing names for gift exchanging. This should be done well in advance of the holiday season. Saves time, money and anxiety.

Decorations: In addition to "decking the halls with boughs of holly," you may want to try these novel decorations.

Candy Cane Vases: Design a festive candy cane vase around a container. Attach candy canes to the outside of the container with florists' clay. Fill with flowers or Christmas greenery. For the finishing touch, tie up your candied vase with holiday ribbon.

candy canes

Stick candy canes to an aluminum can with putty. Fill the can with water, and you have a perfect holiday vase.

Handprint Wreath: Create a hand wreath. Make a pattern by tracing your child's hand onto construction paper. Shape into a wreath (alternate red and green "hands" for Christmas color) by gluing or stapling. See illustration under "Family Traditions" in the Gift section.

PARTIES

TREE TRIMMING

A tree-trimming party is a favorite for all ages. Invite a few guests over to help decorate the tree. Serve hot cocoa and Christmas cookies. Make it festive by playing and singing Christmas carols.

Sparkler: String lights on the tree prior to the party. Save your most fragile ornaments to be added later.

DECORATE IT WITH DOUGH

Ample time needs to be allotted for this party in order to see the dough creations through from start to finish.

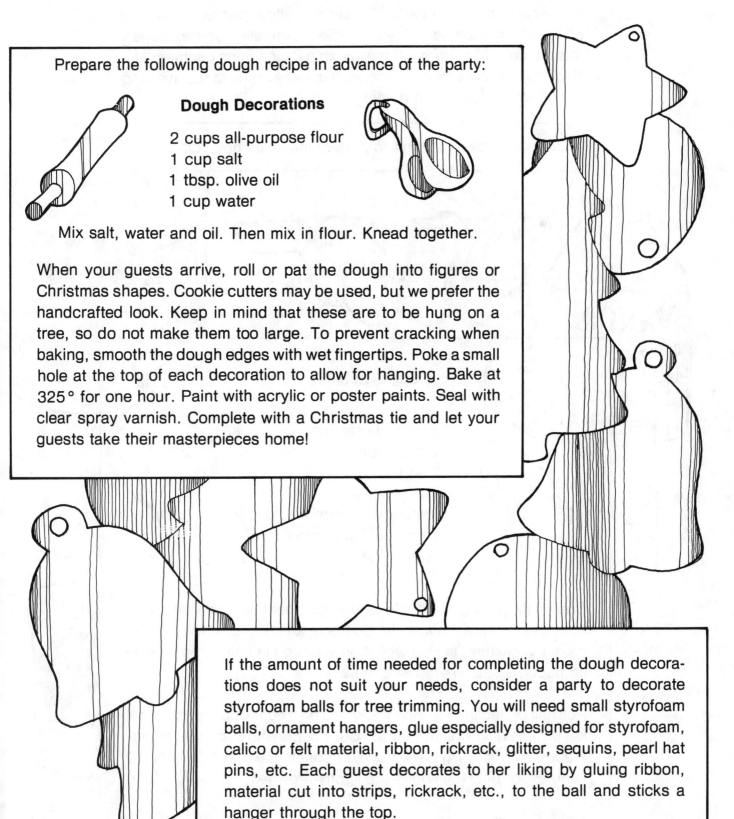

Prepare the following dough recipe in advance of the party:

Dough Decorations

2 cups all-purpose flour
1 cup salt
1 tbsp. olive oil
1 cup water

Mix salt, water and oil. Then mix in flour. Knead together.

When your guests arrive, roll or pat the dough into figures or Christmas shapes. Cookie cutters may be used, but we prefer the handcrafted look. Keep in mind that these are to be hung on a tree, so do not make them too large. To prevent cracking when baking, smooth the dough edges with wet fingertips. Poke a small hole at the top of each decoration to allow for hanging. Bake at 325° for one hour. Paint with acrylic or poster paints. Seal with clear spray varnish. Complete with a Christmas tie and let your guests take their masterpieces home!

If the amount of time needed for completing the dough decorations does not suit your needs, consider a party to decorate styrofoam balls for tree trimming. You will need small styrofoam balls, ornament hangers, glue especially designed for styrofoam, calico or felt material, ribbon, rickrack, glitter, sequins, pearl hat pins, etc. Each guest decorates to her liking by gluing ribbon, material cut into strips, rickrack, etc., to the ball and sticks a hanger through the top.

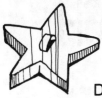

COOKIE DECORATING

Depending on the age group, you may just want to prepare the cookie dough or precut cookies into Christmas shapes and save for decorating at the party. Be sure to allow plenty of working space. In the center of your table assemble cutters, sugar, raisins, colored sugars, chocolate chips, cinnamon candies, etc. Each child decorates her cookies. It is a challenge to resist eating them before they return home!

Sparkler: Provide aprons to protect the little chefs' clothing.

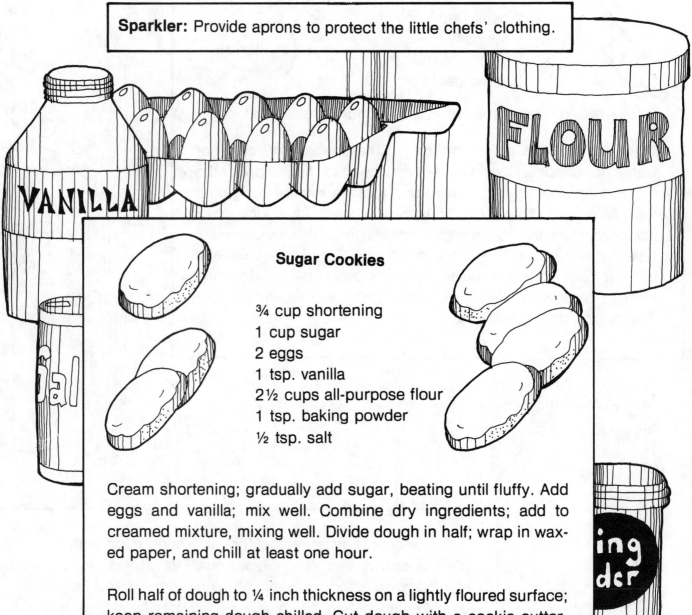

Sugar Cookies

¾ cup shortening
1 cup sugar
2 eggs
1 tsp. vanilla
2½ cups all-purpose flour
1 tsp. baking powder
½ tsp. salt

Cream shortening; gradually add sugar, beating until fluffy. Add eggs and vanilla; mix well. Combine dry ingredients; add to creamed mixture, mixing well. Divide dough in half; wrap in waxed paper, and chill at least one hour.

Roll half of dough to ¼ inch thickness on a lightly floured surface; keep remaining dough chilled. Cut dough with a cookie cutter. Place on a lightly greased cookie sheet; bake at 350° for 12 minutes, or until the edges are lightly browned.

Yield: 3 dozen

SANTA COMES TO TOWN

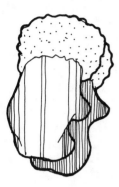

A personal appearance from Santa is the highlight of this evening. Rent a Santa costume and have the adult arrive in a dramatic fashion—in an old car, on horseback, by bicycle or even by sleigh. Any one of these makes a lasting impression. Santa's loot should include a small present for each child, which has been provided beforehand by the parents. Feature Christmas caroling as the final activity on the agenda. As an alternative to caroling, two suggestions are given below to occupy the young guests.

Best Christmas Card

Give each child a piece of construction paper and plenty of markers, crayons, stickers, gummed stars, etc. Fold the paper in half. Have your ''artists'' design a picture on the front and write their own messages inside. Everyone wins. Have plenty of categories: most festive, most colorful, best message, most artistic, most humorous, most original, etc.

Christmas Picture Hunt

Provide the guests with ample copies of old magazines, preferably November and December issues with Christmas themes. Divide the group into teams. Designate hunters and cutters and give a pair of scissors to each team. On a signal, each team tries to assemble as many items as possible from a given list within a limited time period. For your magazine scavenger hunt, include such items as star, bell, Santa, reindeer, holly, snowflake, stocking, ornament, angel, tree, etc. Whichever team collects the most items in an allotted time period wins.

MENU

Visions of sugar plums dance in everyone's head this time of year. Holiday recipes abound. To expand your family favorites, check cookbooks, magazines and food sections of your newspaper. We like the following recipes for their simplicity:

BEVERAGES

Santa Claus Punch

1 package raspberry instant soft drink mix
½ cup sugar
2 cups bottled cranberry juice cocktail
6 cups ice cubes, plus water

In a punch bowl, combine all ingredients. Stir until sugar and drink mix dissolve.

Makes 16—½ cup servings

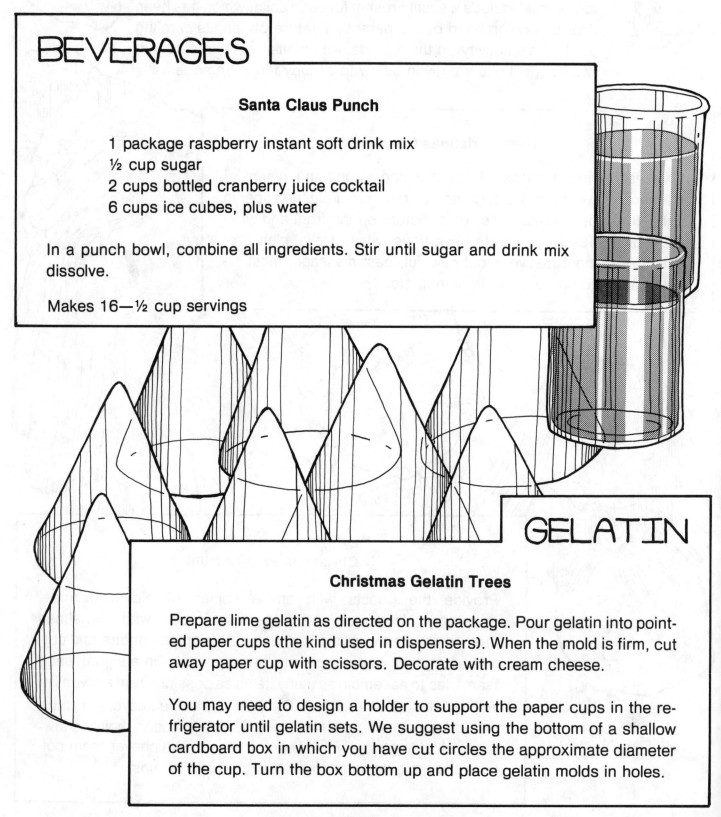

GELATIN

Christmas Gelatin Trees

Prepare lime gelatin as directed on the package. Pour gelatin into pointed paper cups (the kind used in dispensers). When the mold is firm, cut away paper cup with scissors. Decorate with cream cheese.

You may need to design a holder to support the paper cups in the refrigerator until gelatin sets. We suggest using the bottom of a shallow cardboard box in which you have cut circles the approximate diameter of the cup. Turn the box bottom up and place gelatin molds in holes.

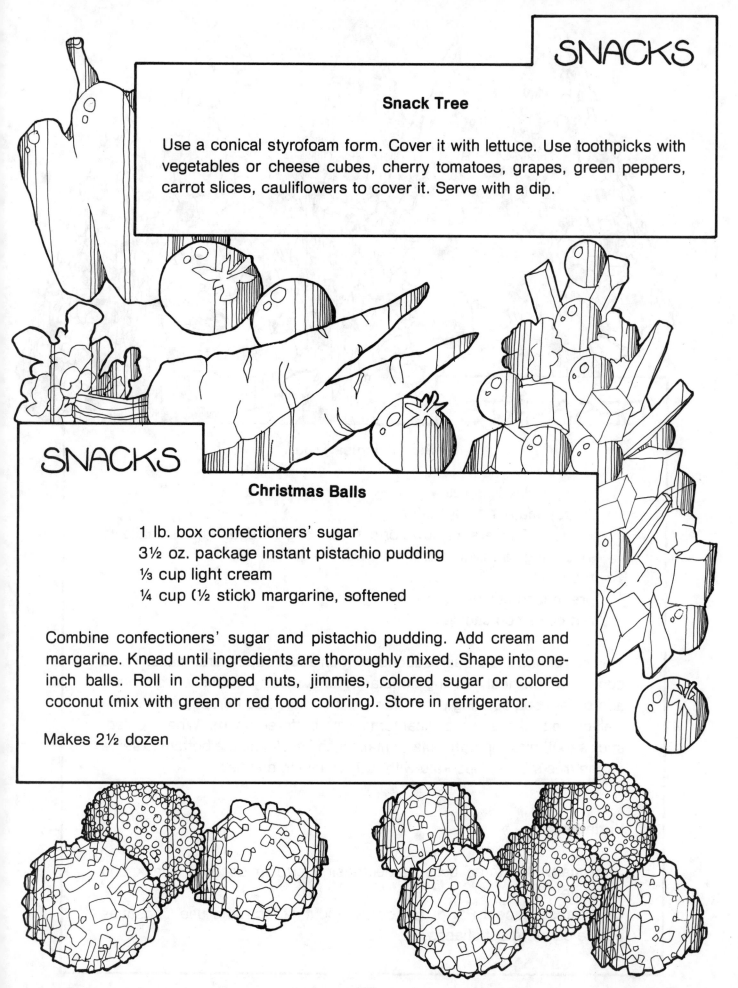

Snack Tree

Use a conical styrofoam form. Cover it with lettuce. Use toothpicks with vegetables or cheese cubes, cherry tomatoes, grapes, green peppers, carrot slices, cauliflowers to cover it. Serve with a dip.

SNACKS

Christmas Balls

1 lb. box confectioners' sugar
3½ oz. package instant pistachio pudding
⅓ cup light cream
¼ cup (½ stick) margarine, softened

Combine confectioners' sugar and pistachio pudding. Add cream and margarine. Knead until ingredients are thoroughly mixed. Shape into one-inch balls. Roll in chopped nuts, jimmies, colored sugar or colored coconut (mix with green or red food coloring). Store in refrigerator.

Makes 2½ dozen

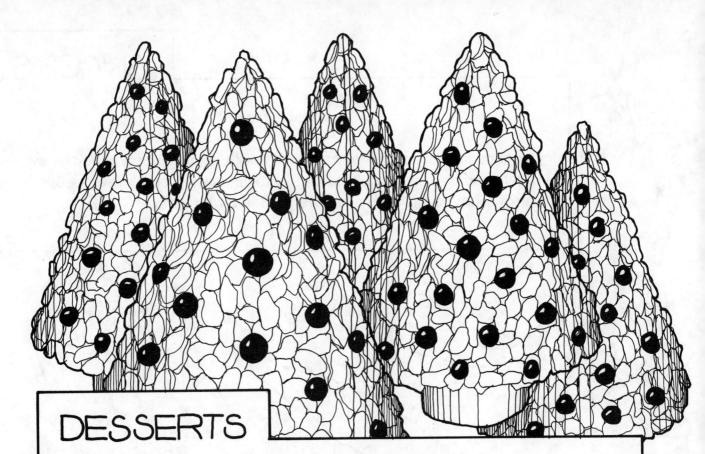

DESSERTS

Rice Krispies Tree

5 cups Rice Krispies
¼ cup margarine or butter
4 cups mini marshmallows or a 10 oz. bag of regular marshmallows
10-12 regular-sized marshmallows
toothpicks
green food coloring
red cinnamon candies

Melt margarine in a 3-quart saucepan, then add 4 cups marshmallows and cook over low heat, stirring constantly until syrupy. Remove from heat; add green food coloring until a fairly dark color. Add cereal and stir until well-coated. Shape into conical forms with buttered hands. When cooled, stick a toothpick through a marshmallow and stick into the bottom to serve as the tree's base. Decorate with red cinnamon candies.

Variations

Snowman: Roll three balls of decreasing size in coconut, stack and decorate.
Christmas Shapes: Pat or roll out to about ¾ inch and use Christmas cookie cutter to cut shapes.

HALLOWEEN PARTY

In a child's mind, Halloween ranks as one of the favorite celebrations of the year. It is the perfect excuse to allow little imaginations to run wild. Whether you raid your attic trunk, buy, rent, or make the costume, your child's delight in dressing up is bound to be contagious. We leave the costume ideas to your imagination, but we offer a couple of hints to make dressing up easier for all.

A word to the wise regarding costume accessories: running with objects such as brooms, swords, magic wands, pitchforks, etc., can be very dangerous. You may want to construct these items from cardboard, foil, paper or other flexible materials. To avoid confusion, tape your child's name to any costume accessories. This makes it easy to identify upon departure from a party.

By burning an ordinary cork (wine bottle type) wonderful masks can be created. After allowing the cork to cool, smudge the face with the blackened end. For fine lines, chisel the end of the cork, then burn. It is great for animal whiskers, mustaches, beards and any facial lines. You will be glad to know that a little soap and water erases every trace!

For theatrical makeup, we recommend that it be removed with baby oil. It is less expensive than cold cream and is usually something you have at hand.

DECORATIONS

To bring out the hallowed spirits, set the stage with dramatic decorations. Cornstalks, carved pumpkins and sheet ghosts are easy to round up.

Try this idea out on your little goblins. Put a piece of dry ice inside your carved pumpkin. Watch the eerie effect as the smoke seeps out of its eyes, nose and mouth. Check the Yellow Pages under dry ice; it is usually available from carbonic companies.

In the center of your table, place a hollowed out pumpkin containing small wrapped favors secured to long ribbons which lead to guests' places. On your signal, children pull their ribbons to reveal their favors.

To raise a chill up your spine, in a dimly lit corner place old costumes stuffed with newspaper. Tie off the arms and legs with string. Stuff a paper bag for the head and draw a face or use a mask.

To cast a spooky glow throughout the house, use orange-colored light bulbs in your lamps. Beware of all ghoulies, ghosties and long-leggedy beasties!

ACTIVITIES

No Halloween party is complete without a dark haunted house. To bring out the howls, a range of scary tricks may be used.

For a spiderweb effect, hang strings from the ceiling to brush across the child's body.

Play tape recordings of spooky sounds: screams, door slamming and creaking, cat howling, fiendish laughter, scary music, etc. (sound effect records are usually available from libraries).

Turn a vacuum cleaner on and off to provide a mysterious roar.

Create a mysterious dead body. Use pillows covered with old sheets to simulate the torso. Direct the child's hands to the individual bowls to feel the organs: ''This is his heart, etc.''

> eyes—peeled grapes
> brains or intestines—cooked macaroni or spaghetti
> heart—Jell-O mold or liver
> tongue—beef tongue
> blood—ketchup

We recommend extra supervision if you undertake this ambitious project.

Apple Bobbing

Pumpkin Piñata: Cover a large balloon with papier mache (newspaper strips dipped in a paste of water and flour), leaving a hole. Paint it orange and decorate with a jack-o'-lantern face. After it has dried, pop the balloon, insert assorted candies through the hole. At this point, you must insert a sturdy string and secure to the piñata by sealing the hole with a strip of papier mache or heavy-duty tape. Hang the piñata from a tree limb, or if indoors, from the top of a doorway or similar stronghold. With blindfold in place, each child takes a turn hitting the jack-o'-lantern with a broom handle or yardstick. Once it has been broken, the children rush in to grab up the goodies!

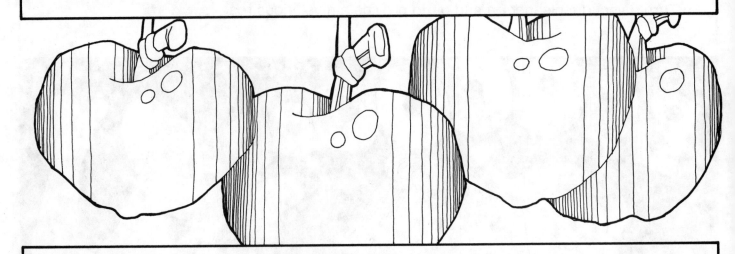

Pumpkin Toss: Cut out a large pumpkin shape from a poster board or any sturdy cardboard. Make fairly large holes for the eyes, nose and mouth. Have children toss beanbags through the openings. Pumpkin-shaped beanbags can be used. You can give points for the most direct "hits."

Musical Pumpkins: Cut out a medium-sized construction paper pumpkin for each child to stand on. Then play as you would for Musical Chairs.

Shoot the Candle: This game is designed for older children and requires extra supervision. Each player is given a squirt gun. The object is to extinguish the flame from a series of candles set at a designated distance from the shooting gallery.

Pin the Hat on the Witch: Play as you would for Pin the Tail on the Donkey. We suggest making a paper hat with each child's name on it to use for pinning.

Trick or Treat Game: Children take turns removing a slip of paper from a container decorated as a jack-o'-lantern. If the slip is marked ''Treat,'' the child receives a candy treat and sits down. If the slip is marked ''Trick,'' the child must perform the stunt written on the paper, for example, cry like a baby, twirl like a ballerina, wind up like a pitcher and throw an imaginary ball, sing a song, etc.

Pumpkin Carving: A pumpkin-carving contest is always a hit with any group. With the younger set, provide magic markers; let them draw the faces, and leave the carving to the parents. For the older group, we offer two alternatives. Instruct each child to bring a carved pumpkin to be judged at the party. Or provide small pumpkins to be carved during the festivities. Prize categories include scariest, funniest, biggest eyes, happiest expression, etc.

Scary Noise Contest: Media buffs will enjoy a scary noise contest. In a separate room, ask each child to record her scariest noise. Play the entire sound tract to the whole group. The child who correctly guesses the identity of each voice wins. Do not forget to keep a list of who's who when taping.

Do not discount the
versatility of the pumpkin!

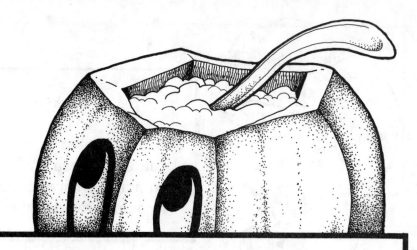

"Pumpkin" Casserole (a sensational serving container)
Clean out the inside of a small pumpkin. Draw a face on the
outside of the pumpkin with magic marker. Prepare squash,
rice or ground beef dish and place inside pumpkin. Bake as
directed and serve in the pumpkin.

Pumpkin Seeds (a delicious healthy snack)
Save and wash pumpkin seeds. Place on a cookie sheet.
Sprinkle with seasoned salt. Bake for 10-15 minutes at 315°.
Tastes similar to sunflower seeds.

Jack-O'-Lantern Salad
Place a circle of shredded raw carrots on each plate.
Decorate with raisins (mouth) and small apple wedges (eyes
and nose) to resemble pumpkin face.

Pumpkin Cup (a fun fruit salad)
Cut the "cap" off an orange. Remove the pulp and fill with
mixed fruit. Faces may be scratched onto the orange with a
ball-point pen.

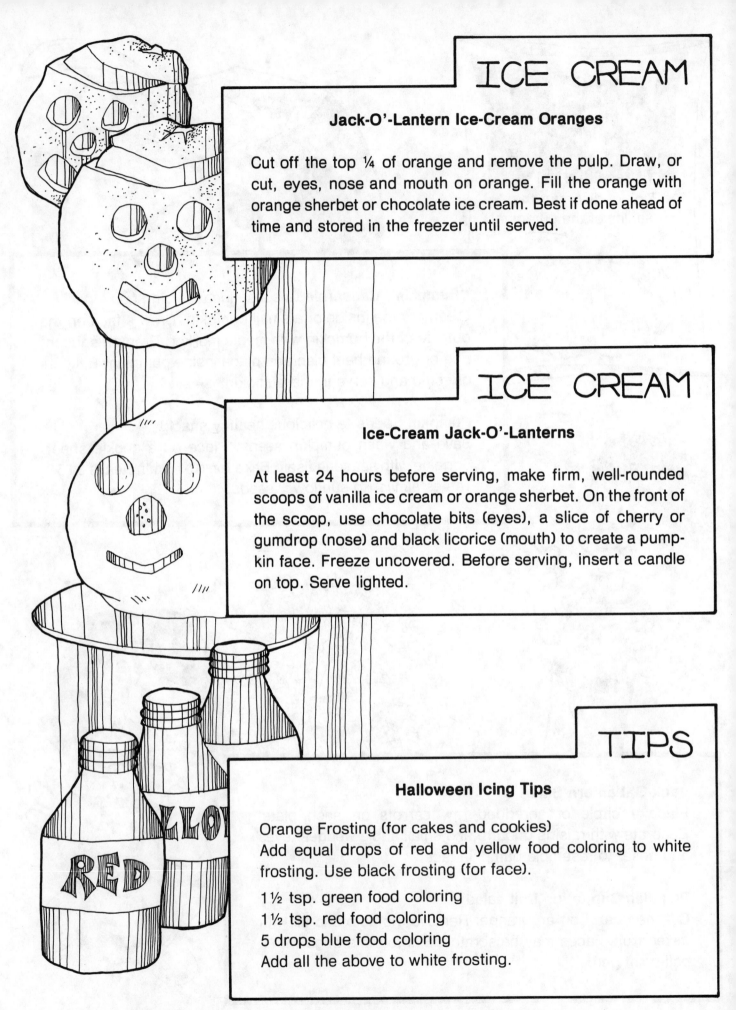

ICE CREAM

Jack-O'-Lantern Ice-Cream Oranges

Cut off the top ¼ of orange and remove the pulp. Draw, or cut, eyes, nose and mouth on orange. Fill the orange with orange sherbet or chocolate ice cream. Best if done ahead of time and stored in the freezer until served.

ICE CREAM

Ice-Cream Jack-O'-Lanterns

At least 24 hours before serving, make firm, well-rounded scoops of vanilla ice cream or orange sherbet. On the front of the scoop, use chocolate bits (eyes), a slice of cherry or gumdrop (nose) and black licorice (mouth) to create a pumpkin face. Freeze uncovered. Before serving, insert a candle on top. Serve lighted.

TIPS

Halloween Icing Tips

Orange Frosting (for cakes and cookies)
Add equal drops of red and yellow food coloring to white frosting. Use black frosting (for face).

1½ tsp. green food coloring
1½ tsp. red food coloring
5 drops blue food coloring
Add all the above to white frosting.

Lollipop Ghosts

Cover a lollipop with white material and tie with yarn at the top of the stick. Draw eyes onto the ghost's head with magic marker.

Draw eyes with marker.

Orange or black ribbon

White fabric or tissue paper

Lollipop stick

VALENTINE'S DAY

The exchange of valentine cards is the most traditional way to celebrate this holiday. If you opt to create your own cards, some useful materials include doilies, red construction paper, lace scraps, photographs, ribbon, stickers, valentine candies, pressed or artificial flowers and fabric swatches. These very special valentines will delight the young artists, as well as the lucky recipients.

Make February 14th a day to remember. While most Valentine's Day celebrations are held at school, you might want to throw your own bash. Turn your fanciful valentine into a party invitation. Fill the party room with festive decorations of red and white: balloons, crepe paper streamers, hearts and cupids.

For an older group of children, this valentine game is worth mentioning:

Tracing Hearts Game

For each child: Cardboard heart cutout
Pencil
Paper

Give each child a precut cardboard heart, pencil and paper. When you give the signal, she is to trace as many complete hearts as possible (without overlapping or going over the edge). The winner is whoever has the MOST hearts on the page in the allotted time, NOT WHOEVER FINISHES FIRST!

Other games to make the party a super success are listed in the section New Approaches to Traditional Games.

Heart Cake

Everyone should know how to bake a heart-shaped cake without purchasing an expensive mold. Bake one eight-inch square cake and one-eight inch round cake. Cut round-cake in half. Place each half on the square cake as shown.

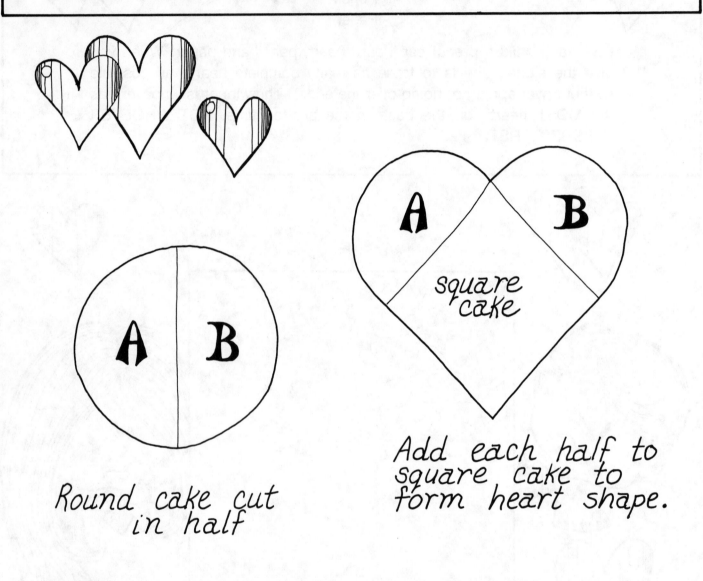

Round cake cut in half

Add each half to square cake to form heart shape.

After icing, you will not see the divisions. Use red or pink icing and spell out your message with heart-shaped candies.

CAKE

Lace Cake: Place paper doily on a pink frosted cake. Sift powdered sugar over doily. Lift very gently.

The highlight of Easter is the traditional dying of eggs followed by a hunt. Packaged dye kits are readily available, but home ingredients can also achieve splendid effects. You will need food colorings and, to personalize the eggs, nontoxic magic markers, ribbon, rickrack, even stickers. Let the eggs soak; turn occasionally for half an hour in bowls of hot water to which food coloring has been added. After the eggs have been colored, let them dry. Egg cartons, paper rolls from toilet paper or paper towels cut into sections make great drying and decorating stands. Decorate eggs with markers, etc. When finished, rub a drop of shortening on each egg to give it a shine and set color.

Egg Dying Party: If you are ambitious, invite a few special friends for an egg-dying party. Hard-boil about four eggs per guest to be dyed and decorated. Award prizes for the most colorful, prettiest, most original, etc. Be sure everyone wins. Let the guests take home their masterpieces in small baskets.

Egg Hunt: What is Easter Sunday without the thrill of an egg hunt? While the chicken is the standard source for eggs, super eggs can be made from Leggs® hosiery containers. Spray them, wrap them with foil, or decorate them to your liking. Stuff these ''bonus'' eggs with goodies and hide along with the rest of the group. Again, give prizes to the guest who finds the most eggs, tries the hardest, finds the most of one color, etc. A functional favor would be a beach pail, basket or plastic watering pail, which can be used for the egg hunt and enjoyed throughout the summer.

Egg Relay: After the hunt, if the troops are restless, an egg relay race is a favorite. Divide the group into teams. Give an egg and spoon to the first person on each team. When the signal is given, each team member must run to a designated point and back without dropping the egg from the spoon. She passes the spoon to the next team member, who then repeats the course. Whoever finishes first wins!

Jellybean Count: Fill a decorated glass jar with jellybeans and tape the number of candies to the bottom of the jar. Let guests try to win the container of jellybeans by guessing the correct number in the jar.

Easter Bonnet: Hats can be made from paper plates. Punch holes on either side of the plate, string through with ribbon and tie under the chin. Color the top and decorate with plastic grass, Easter miniatures, jellybeans, and plastic eggs. After the hats are completed, begin the Easter Parade.

DECORATIONS

If your Easter affair calls for decorations, an egg tree makes a spectacular centerpiece. Decorate a flowering branch with colorful eggs which have been blown out (make a small needle hole at each end of egg; blow out contents). Use glue to attach strings to the decorated eggs and then hang them from the branches. Place this Easter tree in an attractive vase and display in a central location.

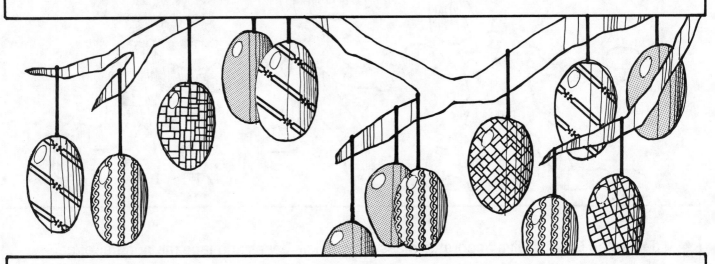

A glass bowl filled with dyed eggs is another effective centerpiece. Easter ''grass'' can be created by cutting thin strips of tissue paper. Use this to display your eggs in the bowl.

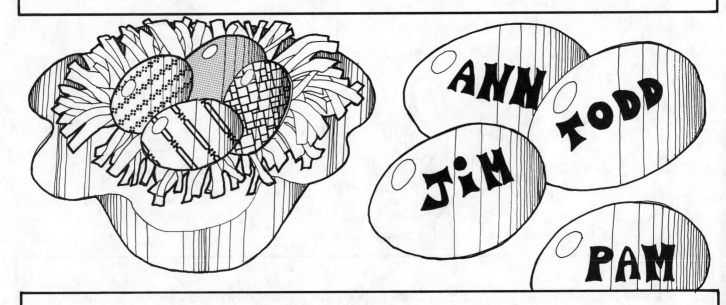

Do not forget that eggs can be used as place cards at your table. Print the name of each guest on a hard-boiled egg with waxed color crayons. Then dye the eggs. The crayoned name will not take the dye, but the rest of the eggshell will.

Here are some unique menu ideas that you may want to add to your traditional Easter fare.

MENU

Bunnies on the Lawn

Dissolve a packet of lime gelatin as directed on the package. Pour gelatin over the bottom of large shallow square dish and chill to set. Place thoroughly drained pear halves, rounded side up, on the gelatin "lawn." Decorate each "bunny": toasted almonds for ears, raisins for eyes, and pieces of candied cherries for tongues. Just before serving, pipe fluffy tails from thick, whipped cream. Cut gelatin in squares, so each guest has a bunny on the lawn.

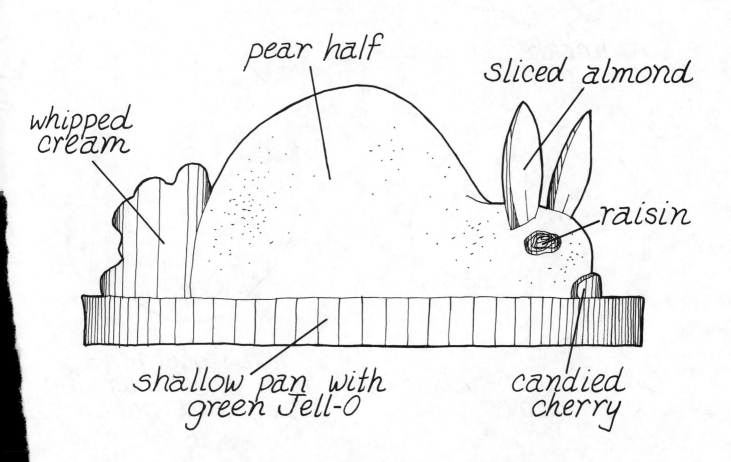

pear half

sliced almond

whipped cream

raisin

shallow pan with green Jell-O

candied cherry

Bunny Biscuits

Using refrigerated biscuits, cut one in half (horizontally) then cut one of these pieces in half to use as the head. Cut the remaining piece in half for ears. Pinch out a bit for the tail and bake as directed.

①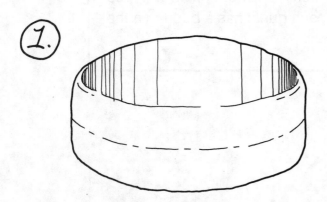

Cut unbaked biscuit in half.

②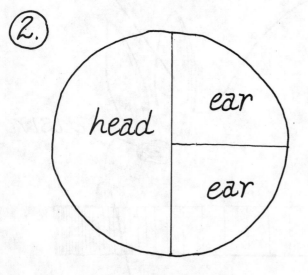

Divide one-half as above

③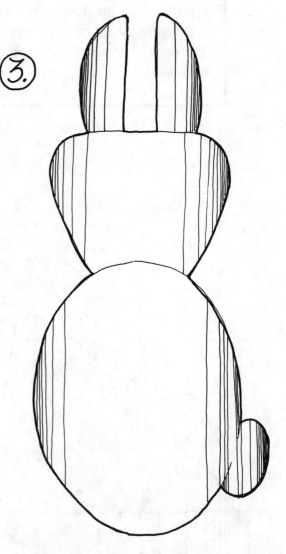

Pinch together – pull a bit out for tail and bake.

DESSERT

Rice Krispie Treats—Bunnies and Eggs

¼ cup margarine or butter
1 pkg. (10 oz.) regular marshmallows or 4 cups miniature
     marshmallows
5 cups Rice Krispies

Melt margarine in a large saucepan over low heat. Add marshmallows and stir until melted. Add Rice Krispies. Stir until well-coated. When cool, using buttered hands, shape 3½ cups of mixture for bunny body and 2 cups mixture for head. Join head and body with toothpicks. Shape remaining mixture into ball for tail. Roll tail in coconut and attach to body with toothpick. Make ears from colored paper. Cut two slits in head to attach ears. Decorate with frostings for eyes, nose, etc.

For eggs: Shape ½ cup mixture into egg shape. Frost or decorate as desired. Makes 10 eggs.

Bunny Cake

All you need is two round cake layers and a lot of imagination for decorating. Cut one layer as shown below. Frost with pink or white icing. Jellybeans are great for the eyes and nose, licorice strips for whiskers, chocolate chips or raisins for the mouth. Sprinkle entire bunny with coconut.

① Round cake for face

② Cut second round as diagrammed

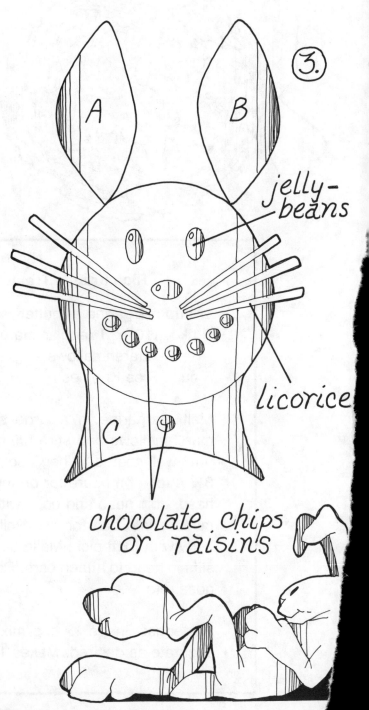

jelly-beans

licorice

chocolate chips or raisins